Wareham's War

(A little town from the Twenties to 1945)

The new South Bridge built in 1927. The old humped-back bridge would never have been able to cope with tanks and other military vehicles of wartime. [Author's collection]

by

Terence Davis

Author of

"Wareham; Gateway To Purbeck"

and

"Arne; A Purbeck Parish In War And Peace

D1583765

Published by Terence Davis,
2, The Oaks, Kitlings Lane,
Stafford, ST17 OLE.

2004

ISBN 0-9547159

Printed by Counter Print
Stafford, Staffordshire.
Tel: 01785 241404

Author's Note

After the publication of *Wareham; Gateway to Purbeck,* I was asked by members of the now defunct Wareham Society to write the continuation of the town's history. This present volume is my fulfilment of their request.

I would like to thank all those Wareham people who over the years have invited me in and talked to me about what they remembered of the town. All have made me most welcome, and for that I am very grateful.

My thanks especially to Hughie Elmes, who kick-started me on this present volume, and to Marjorie Jeffries, who opened the door to a connection with a large number of former American soldiers. To all those who talked to me, or wrote to me, I am greatly indebted. Without them, there would have been no book.

I must thank my wife, Vera, for all her encouragement, both for making suggestions which greatly improve the work and for proof reading.

To all the friends I have made, some now passed away, others happily still with us; to those Americans who have readily answered my questions; and to their comrades who did not survive to see the end of the war, I dedicate this present book.

The author is very grateful to the following people who allowed him to use their treasured photographs;-

Ron Axon, Archie Brennan, Joe Catt, Dan'l Coombes, Hughie Elmes, David Grant, Rev. Basil Watkins-Jones, Butch Jaeger, Doris James, Marjorie Jeffries, Vic and Audrey Lillington, Ray Watkins, The Dorset County Museum and The Imperial War Museum, London.

WAREHAM'S WAR

INTRODUCTION
~ SEPTEMBER 1939 ~

Marjorie Jeffries, née Brewer, in 2002.
[Author's Collection]

Sunday 3rd September 1939; "it is in my mind and it will never go away." Marjorie Jeffries has put into words what that date, now over sixty years ago, meant for her generation.

On a Sunday morning Marjorie was always sent by her father Ted who ran the *King's Arms* in North Street, to get the Sunday papers. Outside the shop, she recalled much later, there were placards announcing "War Declared!"

Mrs Ford was preparing the dinner at *The Yews* while her son Ken was in the dining room with the radio on when Neville Chamberlain, the Prime Minister, spoke telling the nation that the British ultimatum to Hitler over Poland had not been honoured, so Britain was at war.

Jack Tubbs, his wife and his mother were on their way down to Somerset to see an uncle in Chard.

Later that day the Town Crier, Mr. Vincent, went round the streets ringing his bell and shouting that the King was to speak on the radio but "a lot of people didn't have a radio, so we went down to the Town Hall in the evening," recalled Ray Herridge, then a teenager. Inside, Mr. Burt of Burt's Radio in West Street had rigged up a radio. "At the bottom of the stairs was part of the vegetable market and had trestles all round. We youngsters stood on the trestles." The place was packed out. Some would have heard the Prime Minster's speech that morning. Others would have heard it second hand.

"The King spoke. When he'd finished, the radio howled, and old Burt fiddled the knobs, and afterwards, I think it was Alderman Moss, the Mayor, called for three hearty cheers for the King. People stood up and we jumped up and down on the tables! Herbie Brown said, 'Let's have three more!' and we had three more! People threw their hats in the air! We jumped up and down!"

Dan'l Coombes also heard it on the radio. He was with his grandparents down at Slepe, the tiny group of cottages, now almost completely disappeared, near Slepe Farm. As soon as they heard the announcement, the elderly couple wanted to pack him off back to Wareham straight away, fearing perhaps that the Germans were about to invade. "You'd better get home! And they sent me home!" Dan'l recalled.

Like so many of those too young to remember the First World War – some twenty years earlier – Dan'l was puzzled. Again, it is Marjorie who has summed up what many felt. "I knew what was meant but I didn't know how it would affect my life. When I was in the bar I used to hear people talk about the last war."

For adults the British Government's declaration of war did not come totally out-of-the-blue. Newpapers, films and broadcasts had for months been full of German aggression; of the invasion of Czechoslovakia and, later, of Poland; and of the compromise that had been worked out at Munich and the heartfelt relief it brought that war had been averted in 1938. War in that September was not something that came suddenly out of the blue as it did on another September day, 11th, in 2001.

The Government had been making preparations for war for sometime before. Ray Herridge recalled that for several months "we were sticking paper on windows," and the *Dorset County Chronicle* stated that in the month before September 3rd, about 30,000 civilian gas masks had been distributed in Wareham and Swanage. Clearly, war was on most people's minds. Later when the war was declared everyone had to carry their own gas mask. Perhaps, at first, this was a burden but most people soon got used to it. Teenager Harold Rawles used to cycle with his down to Ridge and once as he was peddalling down the Arne road it got caught in the front wheel! And off he came!

In the January of 1939 the county newspaper had commented that improvements were being made to the town's Drill Hall in North Street.

The outbreak of hostilities did mean changes that were to underline to everyone the fact that Britain was at war. About two weeks after the Prime Minister's announcement the *Dorset County Chronicle* reported that the government's blackout restrictions had brought about an earlier closing for most shops in the town. On Mondays, Tuesdays and Thursdays, shops were closing at six o'clock. On Fridays they stayed open for half an hour longer, closing at 6.30pm, while on Saturdays they closed at seven. However fruiterers, tobacconists, confectioners and stationers were closing at seven each night, and at eight on Saturdays.

Even Lady St. Mary's Church services were being affected by the blackout. In November the Rector announced that the evening service would be brought forward to 3.15pm because of the blackout.

Mrs Sellar at the Priory announced within six weeks of the declaration of war that she would start a War Hospital Supply Depot there and requested offers of help with sewing and knitting. Such voluntary groups had been common place in the First World War.

While many were very worried about what might happen during the coming months some like Harry Clark, the former Town Clerk's son, welcomed war. He was very eager to join up. He did not want to miss the action. He had been in the Territorials since 1932 and had risen to the rank of Captain. He was keen to put the skills he had acquired into practice, so he volunteered to be sent to the front.

He was joined by two Wareham district NCOs, Tollerfield, a gardener for the Fillieuls who lived at Sandford House and Harris, a clay pit worker. On 7 January 1940 all three embarked on a troopship to cross the Channel to Cherbourg, then continuing by troop train across France. Leaving this they climbed aboard a cattle truck at 11.30pm, sheltering under a frozen tarpaulin. This took them up toward the front line, near the French/Belgian border.

They arrived at their destination about 12.45am only to find that no one had been notified of their arrival. However one chap, who later became Harry's batman, managed to find Harry a bed in a bungalow belonging to a farm labourer. Thinking of Harry's comfort he put a hot brick in the bed to warm it up but when Harry went up to turn in, he found smoke coming from the bed! Quickly the chap opened the window, threw the brick out and put out any smouldering in the mattress! All this was done without waking the labourer in the next room! Worn out Harry was asleep in no time. His two NCOs were not so lucky. They had to spend the night trying to sleep on some frozen manure in a nearby barn! Both, however, survived! Harry was unable to stand the intense cold of that January/February and having fallen ill was sent home, so he was not at Dunkirk. His two NCOs were not so lucky, but they did come through, unharmed.

In 1939, the older men and women of the town certainly knew what war was like. The First World War was just over twenty years before.

Bert Grant serving in India during the First World War in 1915 - standing on left. [David Grant]

SECTION 1 - Life In The Town Between The Wars.

Chapter 1

Housing and Social Conditions.

To go back in time to the 1930s would be like arriving on another planet. The gulf that separates life at the beginning of the Second Millennium from that of the interwar years is enormous. Computers, CD roms, the internet, fax machines, mobile phones and the like have, in the last decade, completely changed our way of life. Before them came television, automatic washing machines, microwaves, freezers, central heating, supermarkets, the motor car in ever increasing numbers and the National Health Service. The 1930s had none of these. The pace of life was slower and, for most people, life was very much harder.

For many of the Yanks who were suddenly thrust into the town in 1943 Wareham must have seemed primitive and old fashioned .. gas lights in the streets... gas and paraffin lamps in most houses ... houses with stone floors... tarmacked surfaces only on the four main roads... the back lanes still in their more or less natural state.

Yet there had been some important developments going on by 1939. Wareham, like many other towns, had kept up with changes. Any new houses that were built were much better. They had to conform to all the laws being brought in by successive governments. Typical of these were Elm Villas, built just below the North Walls by James Ford of the garage nearby. These had three large bedrooms, with the front one having a superb view over the watermeadows. They had modern flush toilets, admittedly outside in the yard but connected to the main sewers, and that was a great advance. Ford had had them built for his children, and there were other new houses in the town.

Just after the First World War the Borough Council, in common with councils all over the country had tried to ease overcrowding by building its first council houses. Wareham built eleven of them at this time and another fourteen a few years later to provide reasonably good housing for those who were living in what the Council felt was sub-standard accommodation.

One group that would have come into this category was Davis Row, a set of traditional brick and slate terraced houses overlooking the churchyard in Conniger Lane, which formed part of the Rempstone Estate. Six houses, at right angles to

Aerial view of Wareham showing Davis Row on right of picture. [Ray Watkins]

the road, made up the group. During the twenties, when Joan Anderson lived at No.2 with her parents and her siblings, Applelow Orchard and his wife lived next door in the first house. When they left Bill Wheeler and his wife moved in. They were both deaf and dumb. Their son, Wilfred, had a lovely singing voice and sang in the church choir. On the opposite side were Mr. Long and his daughter, with Mrs. Heath beyond them. No.5 was inhabited by Mr and Mrs Bugler, and Mr and Mrs Allingham were in the last house. When they moved out, in came Mr and Mrs John Harris.

Each cottage had virtually only two rooms and there was only one door, the front door. The back wall was plain, unbroken, with no window or door. The one room downstairs had a large open fire that had to heat all the water and on which all cooking was done. A set of chairs, a table and a settee meant the room was also a living room. Beyond this was a little passage that was used on the one side to store coal and on the other for vegetables. A staircase led up to a wide windowless landing where the children slept. Beyond was the bedroom, overlooking the cemetery, which had both a double and a single bed.

The cottages were extremely overcrowded. "The Wheelers, there were four of them; Heaths had four; Buglers had three; Harrises had five; Saunders and his wife; and then we had eight." Twenty-six people sleeping in six bedrooms and six dark spaces at the top of the stairs.

There was no water laid on inside. Instead every drop had to be brought in from a pump that all the cottages shared. Each dwelling had a toilet at the end of

9

its garden on the far side.

In front and at the rear of each property were gardens, and at number 6, Mr Allingham's was large enough for him to be able to keep a pig.

Another row which has also disappeared was Wellington Row, which was off Church Street, at the rear of a terrace of cottages. It was approached through an archway in the cottages on the street. "You went up under the arch and there were three or four cottages. Joe Maker, Polly Hopkinson, and Grannie Allington lived there. The people always kept canaries outside the door, singing away, and always gooseberry bushes outside the door." To young Eddie Anderson, coming under the dark archway and out into the sunlight again "it always seemed nice."

As the cottages in Davis Row began to deteriorate, the Council, in about 1934, decided to move the tenants out. Mrs Wheeler, the Longs, or rather his daughter, who had married after her father's death, the Buglers, and the Harrises all went to Edward's Crescent. Davis Row was pulled down. Mr Pratt built a new house close by and took over most of the former gardens and later Social Services had an office on the site.

The new council houses were designed to be a great advance on the old cottages, with their separate living and dining rooms, kitchen and three bedrooms, but what made each of them luxurious was the provision of an inside, flush toilet and a bathroom.

Ron Axon's parents moved into one of these council houses in 1930. Their's was in Nundico "We were posh," he recalled. "We had our bathroom upstairs!" However, all the hot water had to be carried up as it had only a cold water tap, but this did not detract from the fact it was upstairs, and therefore "very modern!"'

When the Andersons moved in 1935 into a larger house in Mill Lane that had water and electricity laid on, Eddie was over the moon. "The house had bedrooms and an attic, and even the attic had a window! Front door and a back door; doors in between; windows in every room; copper in the kitchen; water inside. It was as if we'd just moved into Buckingham Palace! All of a sudden, you got lights! Pulled a chain and got water!" On the first day he was there, he can remember running all around the house pulling chains and switching lights on and off just for the sheer delight of doing so! "It was marvellous!"

Even so, in spite of all these advantages not everyone who was allocated such a home was as pleased with it as the young Percy Best and his wife, Bess, when they moved into Bells Orchard Lane. Florence Coombes certainly was not. She had grown up in that cluster of overcrowded cottages at Slepe the hamlet beyond Arne, which was a feature of my book on the area, *Arne, a Purbeck Parish In Peace*

The corner of South and East Streets, 1930, taken by Charles F. Metcalfe [DCM]

and War. When Florence arrived in Wareham she missed the family atmosphere of Slepe where all the five families who lived there knew each other very well. In Wareham their spacious garden cut them off from their neighbours and gave her the impression that they were stand-off-ish and cold. Again Florence found the size of the rooms difficult to heat on her husband's meagre wages, compared with what she had been used to, where one kitchen range could warm the whole of the tiny little cottage, and just as important to her, the fuel for that stove was all around her — sticks, branches, peat, furze bushes — and all going for free! In Wareham they had to buy coal. No wonder she did not like the new council houses.

To ease the housing shortage after the First World War some families brought old railway carriages, which were transported and set up on a plot of ground and were turned into comfortable homes. There were examples of these along Nutcracker Lane, in Stoborough and over at Coldharbour.

But whether the house was a new one or one of the older Victorian or Georgian terraces, or even one of the larger houses in the town, the routine for the week was exactly the same. Everyone did their washing on a Monday, never on a Sunday. This was the practice all over Britain at this time, boiling up the soiled clothes in the copper, usually a large iron pot set in bricks with a fireplace below. At Christmas they were the ideal place in which to boil the Christmas puddings! The Grants certainly did this and no doubt they were not alone in doing it. To heat the water most people in the town used coal or, like the Rawles family, wood for this

11

purpose. Jack Tubbs's father used to bring back 'black stocks', the blackened branches of furze bushes, and others did the same since they could be found in abundance on the heathland all around the town. It had to be the blackened branches, the ones that had survived a heath fire and not ones that were still green. Those just would not burn. Dan'l Coombes' family certainly burnt furze wood at Slepe, after all it was all for free. Mr. Tubbs brought his back from around Sandford Pottery where he worked.

Washing went on all day. For the Andersons and the other inhabitants of Davis Row it was a much more difficult task. They had no sink inside the cottage so everything had to be taken outside and washed in a bowl on a stool in the open, tolerable on a sunny summer's morning, but thoroughly unpleasant on many a cold Monday morning. Then mother had to set her bowl on the table indoors. Eitherway, the clothes had to be scrubbed and washed by hand. Since none of the cottages that made up the Row had an inside tap every drop of water had to be collected from the standpipe in the yard. These were only turned on for three hours each day. If it was frosty the first person up in the Row had to thaw the pipe out. Eddie recalls on many cold mornings in winter seeing burnt bits of newspaper blowing about in the yard.

After all the clothes had been boiled they were rinsed in fresh water into which Reckitt's Blue had been mixed. Then they were mangled and hung up to dry. This was fine if it were a good sunny or windy day; much more difficult if it was raining. Then the dripping clothes had to be dried indoors as best they could.

Next came ironing, with flat irons heated on the kitchen range, trying not to get them too hot or picking up 'smuts', specks of dirt from the range. That took up most of Tuesdays and the rest of the week was spent, among other things, in repairing clothes to make them last longer. Socks had to be darned. Maud Norris spent a large part of her childhood doing this.

Most kitchen floors were still stone and therefore needed scrubbing and whitening regularly. On top most families had coconut matting and rugs. The front room,if there was one, was still kept for special occasions, Christmas, wedding parties, funerals, the rare events when the fire was lit. Here the floorboards were probably covered in linoleum (lino for short), and carpets on top of it.

The large cast iron kitchen range was more or less universal for cooking and heating water. There was always a kettle on top, observed Harry Rawles, which was kept going all day long, even in summer. Regular polishing of the range with blacking was required to keep it shining and its hearth needed whitening just as frequently. David Grant recalls that on one Sunday morning his mother had done this little job and had lit the fire in the range. Sometime later she went to open the door of the oven next to the fire to see if it were ready for the Sunday joint, when out of the oven shot the cat! It jumped straight out of the open window and the Grants never saw him again!

Repairs were usually done using whatever was at hand; for instance, when the cold water tap over the scullery sink began to leak Jim Tubbs got an old bicycle tube and cut it into strips. These he wrapped around the leak and held them in place with two bits of wire. "That held for years!" his brother Jack recently recalled.

In spite of low wages most families would have considered their standard of living as acceptable. Joan Anderson summed it up for everyone when she said; "We had a good life and a wonderful mother. We never went without. There was always food on the table! When we used to come home from school, we were pleased to go home to an old fashioned stew – rabbit stew, and an old fashioned spotted dick with jam or honey – always done in a clean pillowcase and put in a saucepan. A piece of pork or beef on Sundays."

Food, basic though this may have been, was not scarce. Houses had long gardens and it was the husband's job to produce as much as he could to feed his family. "Everyone's backgarden was their vegetable garden." (Beryl Binding) Many men also had allotments. These and the gardens meant a constant supply of fresh vegetables and fruit. In an age before freezers, potatoes, when dug up, would be stored, as Beryl explained, "dad would dig a hole in the garden and put the potatoes

South Street [Author's Collection]

13

in, with straw on them and earth over the top." This was a time-honoured method that was used all over the country. Carrots were stored similarly but in sand. "People with fruit trees gave you apples and plums and there was blackberrying; so we did alright." This last comment from Beryl just about sums sit up. Food was certainly not plentiful or particularly varied, but no one starved.

Beryl's family were luckier than some. Their father went shooting regularly with Farmer Gover for rabbits, which was their main stay. Occasionally, they had deer which were shot up at Grange.

In addition families would exploit what was available around the area; for instance Harry Rawles and his family used to go down to Redcliffe or to Russel Quay at Arne and row over to one of the islands, Long or Green, and search for seagulls' eggs. They took a couple from each nest. There were usually about four in a nest. These were then carefully taken back home where they were preserved in eisenglas until they were needed.

Older folks still remember the bakeries that the town had – Bennetts of East Street and Bowles and Spencers of Brixey's Lane. "Such lovely bread," Beryl said, referring to the latter. "On Good Friday you hung up a bag on your door and he'd (the Bowles and Spencer roundsman) come early and put hot-cross-buns in it."

Though bakeries were within easy reach, Wareham was still old-fashioned enough for many women to bake their own bread. Mrs Rawles was one of them. In addition, she also made some of her own cheese. "There weren't many times when there wasn't a bag of sour milk hung on top of the tap in the shed for making cheese. Milk went off quickly in those days and mum would put it into a muslin bag and tie it on. All the juice used to drip out of the muslin into the sink, leaving the cheese inside."

Bath night was, at least for the children, a constant source of delight. Except in the newer council houses and some of the larger properties, this meant bringing in a large tin bath which was placed in front of the fire. Often this was done on a Monday night when there was plenty of hot water in the copper left over from boiling the clothes. The Rawleses and the Tubbses, however, lit up their coppers specially on Fridays for their baths, and they were not alone in doing this on that night. Then the hot water had to be ladled out into the bath. For the Andersons in Davis Row bath night involved even more effort, for all their hot water had to be heated up in saucepans on the fire.

Even in their new council house, where they had a bathroom, the Bindings did not have hot water upstairs so all the water had to be heated on the range in the kitchen and taken up in buckets. As a result, they often washed in cold water, Beryl

14

Harold Rawles, 2002
[Author's Collection]

recalled.

However the water was heated, the evening gave endless fun to the children. When it was all over the bath had to be emptied. Harry does not recall seeing his parents ever having a bath but he recalls them using cans to get the water out of the bath. This was very slow and laborious. Other families used large buckets. The water was then carried out and tipped onto the garden. When all this had been done, Harry's parents took their bath out into the yard and hung it up on its nail and all over Wareham many others did likewise.

By modern standards, of course, many toilets in the town were still primeval! Wareham had no sewage system until 1925. Before this, and for a long time afterwards, most houses had a bucket in an outside shed; the 'thunderbox' was how the Govers of Redcliff referred to theirs. Getting rid of its contents was a task that many did for themselves. Jack Tubbs's father, for example, "disposed of it in that he had a garden down the road (in Church Street)." Over at Ridge Harold Rawles's grandfather dug a hole in his garden and tipped the sewage in. When the hole was filled he covered it with earth and planted marrows on top! "Great marrows!" comments Harold today! His Uncle Bill even got into the Guinness Book of Records for the size of his marrows!

If a household could not, or did not want to have the bother of emptying their privy themselves, then the sanitaryman, George Cox, would come and empty the bucket into his cart, provided, of course, a sixpence (2 1/2p.) was left on the toilet seat. He started on his rounds about half past four each day. He was a great character, who could not read or write, yet he was a very acute businessman.

Herbie Elmes used to tell a story;—

A newcomer to the town once approached George, "Mr. Cox, the sanitary engineer?"

"Yes, ma'am," he said, "What do you want?"

"Would you come round and see to the bucket for me?"

"Yes, ma'am. Tuesdays and Fridays, I'm that way."

"Perhaps Fridays."

"That's alright then."

"Can you let me have the account in once a month, or once every three months?"

"Ma'am, you leave the tanner (6d, or 2 1/2p.) on the seat. If the tanner ain't on the seat, the bucket ain't emptied!"

Those who lived on St. John's Hill were fortunate. They had a back entrance to their property and Coxey could come in the back way, empty their toilet and go. Those houses without a back entrance were not so fortunate. Even "if you were in the sitting room and had visitors, it made no difference (to Coxey). He'd go through and get it. If he couldn't get to it he wouldn't come back again" at a more convenient time! (Eddie Anderson)

Of course it was an age before Andrex and soft toilet rolls, so many people tore up old newspapers and hung the pieces on a nail in the toilet. Harry Rawles much preferred The *Daily Sketch* to other newspapers as it "was the softest of the lot!" His grandparents did this at Ridge but it could be very frustrating as Harry now recalls. As a young lad he often found "something of interest in a bit of torn paper and then you'd try to find the rest of it, the bit that mattered, and you'd never find it!"

After a mains sewage system came to the town from about 1925 things gradually got more hygienic as many houses were connected up with the main sewer. Jack Tubbs's home in Ropers Lane was certainly up-to-date in this respects, so too were the new council houses, but even here the toilet was not indoors. "You had to go out and round the house. You used to take a torch with you." (Beryl)

In the interwar years life still had one foot firmly in the past in many ways. Harry's grandmother still wore long black skirts and an old black spotted apron down to her heels and his father never went anywhere without his hat. Even later in life, after Harry had married and went with his wife to see his parents, "he'd always put his hat on before he came to the door to see us off," nor did he take his coat off on the beach. Most elderly people at this time did not.

Sunday morning was a ritual; everything at home spick and span; church, or chapel, in the morning; roast beef for lunch and a walk in the afternoon. For the Rawles family this meant along the river to Ridge where they would have their sandwiches and then walk back. It was virtually the same for the Tubbs's but usually they came back through Redcliffe and Stoborough where father would have a pint. Mrs Rawles always stuck to a glass of lemonade and the children had a bag of crisps. For young Ray Herridge it involved going down to Swineham and back round to Bestwall. "Before the war you could walk through the Granary, through a doorway at the far end and along in front of the boathouse. Then in front of Mr. Sturdy's boathouse and then half round the house, through the Priory gate, which used to be there but has now vanished and along in front of the Priory." Alternatively if they wanted a shorter walk they would go down to Little Quay, a favourite place for picnics, he recalls. It was wide enough for several people to sit down. From here Ray and the ladies who fostered him could cross in front of the Priory and came back round the cemetery into Connigar Lane. From here there was a choice of whether to go straight back home or walk along the walls. Such was the ritual of Sundays before the war.

School dominated most children's lives. The Church of England School where most of the town's children went was in Bonnett's Lane. The early history of this institution has been fully dealt with in *Wareham, Gateway to Purbeck*.

Until 1939 it was an all-age school taking children from four or five right through until 14. At the age of eleven they could take the 11 Plus Examination for a place at Swanage Grammar School and Vic Lillington was one of the few who gained a place there.

However keeping him there was not at all easy for his parents. All the boys there had to wear a uniform but the clothes could only be purchased at one shop, Sydenham's of Swanage. Vic can still quote the prices of some of the things he had to have; his cap cost five shillings (25p.), his tie two shillings and sixpence (12 1/2p.) and his football shorts, which were obligatory, another 7 shillings and sixpence (37 1/2p.) In addition he had to pay five shillings a term (25p.) to play sports and this was not optional.

In view of all the expense of keeping a boy at Swanage Grammar many parents prayed that their child would not pass the scholarship. Even boys who won this honour might not be allowed to take it up. The parents of a friend of Vic's turned down their son's place arguing "We can't afford to let him go." Others, like John Symonds' dad, saw grammar school education as the key to higher paid jobs and a secure future.

For Vic and John going to Swanage involved hard work which tended to cut them off from their contemporaries. It meant a train ride to and from Swanage each day, lots of homework and less time to spend with their former mates. However, the daily train journey did have its compensations. John confessed that he could usually complete his homework before he got home!

Vic Lillington, 1929 scholarship boy to Swanage Grammar School when it first opened.
[Vic Lillington]

For those who, like Vic's friend, were not allowed to go and for all those who were not awarded scholarships, that is the great majority of children, they stayed in Wareham at their existing school. These, like those all over the country, were catering for children from infancy right through to fourteen, the age when they could leave and find a job.

But by 1939 things were beginning to change to give older children a secondary education more fitting to their age. In that year Dorset County Council began building a school for those eleven years olds who did not go to a grammar school. This was the Secondary Modern School up the Worgret Road. It was due to have its first intake of pupils in September 1939.

For those who did not want to stay at their elementary school and whose parent could afford it there was 'Pinkie' Skewes' School in North Street. The early history of this has been dealt with in *Wareham, Gateway to Purbeck'*. Bob Thompson went there, as did Doris Fooks. She was one of five girls there in the thirties. Apart from Mr. Skewes, of course, who taught the older class, there was one other teacher, a little tiny man with a bald head. He taught the younger class, but used to wear small trousers, which, according to Bob, made him look, in the eyes of the pupils, like Rupert Bear! The two classrooms were still divided by a curtain, which on Saturday mornings was drawn back so 'Pinkie' could take every pupil. Miss Lucas came in regularly to teach the piano. Enterprisingly, perhaps, 'Pinkie' used to teach shorthand, Pitman's Shorthand.

According to Bob, Lawrence of Arabia was a frequent visitor to the school, on Saturday mornings, when he came to collect two of the lads. "He did this for perhaps half a dozen times over two or three years."

All 'Pinkie' Skewes' washing was done by Audrey Richards' grandmother. Audrey was, she confessed recently, "a little scared of old Mr. Skewes. He had a hat and gown on."

"I am told by your grandmother, Audrey, that you like reading," he said on one occasion when she went to take the washing back.

"Yes, I do. I do a lot."

"Can you tell me anything about Lawrence of Arabia?"

"Wasn't he killed in a road crash.?"

"Do you know what he was?"

"Wasn't he an archaeologist? I don't know what it means!"

"Right! You've got it! Come into my study.' He was leaving the school shortly, and he gave me a book that belonged to Lawrence!"

Both stories remind us that Lawrence was quite well known in the town at this time and when he was killed, several people remarked on how there was only one topic of conversation in the town after the event.

There were one or two real characters about then. There was Old Albert and his wife, Lil, who used to live in a gravel pit down on the Common. Albert used to do odd jobs around the town. He would do anything and on occasions would even blow the church organ. If someone did not turn up, then one of the choirboys had to do it! "You had to pump like anything," recalled Herbie Elmes, "to keep the weight up and then you could have a rest. For little boys, it was hard going, and if the organ was playing 'Onward, Christian Soldiers!' it could finish up like bagpipes with no wind." Albert often did not turn up when he was supposed to.

Another character was Jesse Green who also did odd jobs. He lived in a hut on the banks of the Frome, a little upstream of the town.

Rainbow Cafe at No.3 North Street, owned by Betty Monk in the 1930's. [Author's Collection]

Chapter 2
Work

By the time the Yanks arrived in Wareham, the unemployment problem had been solved. Men over 18 were in the army, and the war effort provided a tremendous demand for labour. But before that, in the twenties and thirties, Wareham suffered, as other places did from the depression and lack of jobs. Eddie Anderson commented that 1929 to 1930 , and 1933 to 1934, were "pretty hard times."

David Grant's father had returned from the army after the First World War, hoping to go into the policeforce, but he had contracted malaria when he was sent with his regiment to India, and that ruled the police out for him. He was very frustrated and returned to his old job in Bowles and Spencer's bakery.

Jack Tubbs' father was out of work about 1926. He turned up at Wareham Market and found that someone was needed to drive four heifers from the market all the way to Studland. When he had done this, he had to walk all the way back to Wareham, but he got a crown (5 shillngs/25p.) for it. Jack remembers he "was as pleased as punch with it."

With so much difficulty in getting a job, it is not so surprising that one lad began to think of going abroad and trusting his luck in what was then the Empire. At the age of fifteen, Charlie Dame, was lured by the prospect of life in Canada. This was part of a government scheme to encourage young people to seek a new life abroad. Thus, his passage across the Atlantic was paid for, on condition he stayed two years. Charlie was the only one who went from Wareham and had to go all the way to London on his own. At Waterloo, he met others and they went up to Liverpool together. Here more joined them. From here they sailed to Belfast, where more were picked up and then came the long trip across the Altantic. When they did get across, the St. Lawrence River was frozen so they landed at Quebec.

Charlie spent the next two years working in Montreal, before getting a job with Stephen Letts and his wife. They were a remarkable pair, for both were deaf and dumb but were still able to run a farm. Later, he worked for a time with Clifford Cox and his brother. However, Charlie was far from happy and in 1928 he returned to England and landed at Southampton. His was a notable experience, not unique, but interesting because he did not settle in Canada. For him, the scheme was not successful, but were there others for whom it opened up a new world? How many settled? How many returned?

From an early age, of course, children in the town, as elsewhere, were expected to help their parents, mending and preparing meals for the girls, and gardening for both sexes. David Grant did all kinds of jobs for his grandfather. Once he had to put in a new pane of glass in his greenhouse and putty it and all. This was at the time, he recalls, a new experience for him. Audrey Richards, just outside the town, was expected to collect the dirty washing in her dolls' pram for her grandmother from her customers all around the area , and, when she had washed and ironed it, deliver it back again.

For most children there was no opportunity to stay on at school. Only the odd one, like Vic Lillington, passed the 11 Plus exam and went to Swanage Grammar School. A few affluent parents could afford to send their children to private or boarding schools.

For the rest, the overwhelming majority, it was a job at 14. For many boys this was perhaps not such a big step as many already had a part time job. Harold Rawles had already been delivering meat for the Co-op for two years before he reached his leaving age. He arrived at the shop at 8 in the morning on Saturdays and worked until 4 in the afternoon. For this he earned 5 shillings (25p). The first day he went, he found the tray of meat too heavy to carry to the bike, and, even worse, to get it into the basket on the front of the delivery boy's bike, while trying to hold onto the bike. The difficulty was overcome by two of the men carrying it out.

"Well!" Harold recalls saying, "That's alright! You're doing that here, but what am I going to do when I get to the first house in Stoborough? How am I going to get off the bike then? If I've got to balance it now, how am I going to get off?"

"Well," one of the two men said, "there's a stand on the front. Just kick it down and pull down on the handle bars and it'll stand up!"

And that worked. Harold set off and delivered all round Stoborough and Furzebrook, out to the claypits and back round Ridge to the town.

On another occasion, he recalls it was very cold and icy and when he was going down over the railway bridge, he skidded, and came off his bike. The meat was flung all across the road! In panic, he hastily gathered it all up and cycled over to his granny at Ridge. There she washed the joints and stuck the labels back on where they thought they should go, and Harold was off to deliver them.

Before he left school, Ray Herridge used to go with the milkman on his rounds and help ladle the milk out into people's jugs. One port of call was John and Sybil's boathouse, a barge with a little house on top, which was moored upstream.

"Everyday I walked up there with a pint of milk. One day, when I was going over the bridge, I saw the boat adrift. I ran back up to the police-station, and said, 'The John and Sybil boathouse is drifting!' But they threatened to throw me in the cells for wasting their time! But when they came down and saw it, they said I'd done it, but I hadn't! It broke away during the night and drifted. It was pulled back again."

At other times Ray would accompany the piano tuner, old Johnny Lucas, when he went out tuning organs. Often, Johnny, or 'Bunny' as he was known, could be seen about the area riding his belt driven Sunbeam motorcycle in his bowler hat; "always his bowler hat!" (Ray). While 'Bunny' was at work, he found Ray very useful keeping the organ pumped up. He also helped George Cox clean out his woodshed down on Abbot's Quay and went as a delivery boy for the wool shop in North Street, next to the *King's Arms*. For this he received 3d(1p), which he was pleased with. It meant he could go to the pictures for 2d and have a pennyworth of broken biscuits as well!

Herbie Elmes was another delivery boy, taking letters along the towpath down towards Ridge, where there were several house boats. A Mr. Friedemann lived in one. He was an artist and one day when Herbie went along and opened the door, he caught sight of a lady in the nude! Astonished, he made a hasty retreat! Later, at the age of 12 during the First World War, he was delivering bread for Bennetts, as well as going to school. Every day he had to carry the loaves down to Bestwall Farm and once a week he had to push a truck loaded with flour sacks for the Bennetts ovens. When the army camp was set up on the Worgret Road he had to push the truck up to the officers' mess there. Sometimes, the officers invited him to stop and have dinner with them, but he could not. This journey had to be done during his lunch hour from school. For all his efforts before and after school and till 7 or 8 on Fridays and all day Saturday till 10 o'clock at night, he received 3 shillings (15p.) a week.

When he had been at the bakery for about eighteen months, his mother said he must ask for a rise, adding that if he did not she would ask as she felt 3 shillings a week was ridiculous for all the things he was asked to do. Finally, Herbie plucked up enough courage to ask. Mr. Marshallsay was the manager there, as the two Bennett brothers had retired by that time. He was a large man, and Herbie always found him rather pompous.

"Come in! What do you want, Elmes?"

"I've been here now so long," the lad began, "and I think perhaps I ought to have a little more money."

"I'm glad you've come. We're taking on a full-time boy. Take a week's notice!"

Jack Tubbs was another who became an errand boy, delivering groceries and meat for Dickers in West Street. He had a similar starting time to Harold, eight in the morning but finished two hours later, at six each night. His was for a six days week, not just on Saturdays, as Harold's was. For this he received, in 1936 when he first started, 13s (65p.)

Similarly, Ron Axon went to work while he was still at school. He was an evening delivery boy for the Co-op, cycling out to Trigon and Carey to the north and west, Stoborough to the south, and Bestwall in the east. "I left when I was twelve and a half, and went to work with Mr. Joy." His outfitters business still proclaims his name in North Street. "He was a sick man. I used to come from school, go there, and, when I got there, he used to go upstairs and lie on his bed, leaving me in charge!" Looking back now, Ron is surprised that a twelve and a half year old was left in charge of the till and the shop. He learned how to serve customers, taking "out all the socks from the case and show people. When they'd gone, I'd have to fold them all up again. I ran the shop, and packed up all the shirts properly!"

For many, when they did leave school at 14, there was not much choice. Between the wars was a time of great unemployment everywhere, and jobs were hard to find. Marjorie Jeffries still remembers the unemployment office. "You had to go through a little passage where you had to go to get the dole, about halfway up West Street, by Roses, the butchers. I remember seeing the dole queue right down that road and round the corner. Unemployment was that bad."

Perhaps, the situation in Wareham being on the south coast was not so bad at this time as some places. At least that is what miners from South Wales and the Forest of Dean thought. Several miners came to the town in the 1920s, searching for work. Wareham men were far from happy at this, for the miners were glad of anything since there was little work in the South Wales coalmines. They would work for labourers' wages. "Skilled bricklayers working for labourers' wages, just to get a job. Bosses sacked their own men who had been there

A well-known landmark, the tower of the Pottery [Rev. Basil Watkins-Jones]

23

for a long time."

Ray Watkins' father came from the Forest of Dean with his brother looking for work, but they were advised that if they wanted work they would have to go to London. Ray's father took the advice, but his brother returned home. However, Ray and his wife did not like the capital and came back to Wareham. Here, he worked whenever he could get something to do, sometimes for

The wagon in Sandford Pottery [Rev. Basil Watkins-Jones]

the council, sometimes for the gravel company, and sometimes for Rempstone Estates. It was not until 1936 that he got a permanent job, at Sandford Pottery.

Here, he may well have met Jack Tubbs' father, who was employed packing the earthenware pipes in heather to prevent them being damaged. They were then put in a railway wagon. When this was full, a couple of shire horses pulled it on railway lines down to the mainline.

Sandford Pottery was an important employer in the area. It had been established in the 1850s. One story goes that it had been started by Lady Angela Burdett-Coutts as one of her schemes for encouraging industries to offset the unemployment of the 1840s. While Edna Healey, whose biography of Lady Angela is outstanding, could not confirm this story, she did say that such a foundation was typical of much of Lady Angela's work.

By the 1930s, therefore, it had been established some eighty years and had a good reputation for its products, earthenware pipes for use as sewers or for water and hand-made bricks. It had, however, become very old fashioned in its production methods.

Herbie Elmes was one of those who worked at the pottery, although it was after the Second World War when he went there. The conditions he recalled suggested that little had changed since the factory had started, let alone since the inter-war years.

It was run by Captain Shaw, who had been a captain in the First World War. He lived at Swanage, and his two sisters at Camp Cottage, almost across the road from the pottery. Herbie remembered the ex-Captain as an efficient manager, but one that was rather sarcastic.

There was no china clay on the site. Originally, this used to come from a pit on the Morden road. By Herbie's time this had long been abandoned, as had the making of china tableware. Instead, the company had turned to making earthenware pipes. For this, they could use local clays from near the Holton Heath railings, and shale from Kimmeridge.

Wheelbarrows, pushed by hand, were used to carry the clay and the pipes around the site. "One chap collapsed out right. They pushed him down on a wheelbarrow to one of the houses. Forever after that the barrow was known as the 'Tory Ambulance'

"Mr. Pope was putting in a machine and the chain slipped, shook the whole place and brought down a lot of dust. Mr. Shaw rushed out of his office and demanded to know what was happening. The lathe was still going round and swinging and hit Mr. Pope on the leg!" That story of Herbie's probably dates from after he joined he factory in 1946, but it illustrates the primitive conditions there.

Perhaps a typical example was that Captain Shaw refused to have electricity to light the premises. Instead, the main workshops were still lit by duck lamps, which "gave out a little glow. –three or four round the brick kiln, all smoking away. They were paraffin lamps." (Herbie Elmes) Kilns were fired by coal, Welsh coal. In each corner of the kiln was a fireplace, where "you put the coals in, and cover that up, and gradually build the fire up." If one of the kilns needed repairing, it had to be shut down.

If the Board of Trade Inspectors were due, Herbie was instructed to cover all dangerous machinery left over from the war.

In spite of all this, the factory, said Herbie, had a "happy little family atmosphere." For example, the workforce used to go over to the kitchen of the house (Camp Cottage).

For boys, the basic choice was between the claypits and Holton Heath. Dan'l Coombes, in 1944, chose the former, but, really, he did not have a choice. His relatives were already there and the wages were

Part of Sandford factory with pottery moulds [Rev. Basil Watkins-Jones]

good. Miss Bussell did offer to teach him the grocery trade, but his mates were already up at the claypits. Miss Bussell paid him 40 shillings a week (£2), whereas at the claypits he would be getting double, £4. So, for him, there was little choice.

Perhaps it was easier for boys to find work. They were cheaper than adult men. Many were taken on full time where they had been working.

For Harold Rawles this was at the Co-op. He now worked every day, except, of course, Sundays and he had a half day off on Mondays. For this he received 14 shillings a week (70p), but he was not happy at the Co-op. It was not the wages, but the butcher who he found was a difficult chap to get on with, always swearing and cussing, even when customers were present. That

The kilns in Sandford Pottery works
[Rev. Basil Watkins-Jones]

Harold did not like, so after sticking it for nine months, he went on with his dad, who drove a dust-cart with a trailer on the back for Tatchell's of Sandford. He used to go collecting paper and rags around the area. Harold was useful to him for getting up in the trailer and sorting the waste out for him before they went back to the depot at Westport House. His father also found him useful in another way. When he reached Tyneham he was supposed to let the boss know he had arrived in that village and he disliked using the telephone, still an unfamiliar invention to many at this time. If Harold was with him, he would ring up from the box that is still preserved at Tyneham.

At the age of 16 Harold learned to drive one of the lorries that were used to collect the hay during the haymaking season. He evidently drove well and his boss noticed his skill.

"Would you like to take the lorry on

Mr Coombes and his four sons -
Kenneth, Dan'l, Edwin and Alan.
[Dan'l Coombes]

the road?" he suggested one day.

"But I'm not old enough!" gasped the astonished Harold.

"Well, you're big enough!" came the reply.

"Well, OK! I'll take it out!"

His boss found him some L plates, and he drove up to the gravel pits without anyone supervising him! When he arrived, he asked the foreman where to go.

"See that gravel? Get up on top, and throw it up in the lorry!"

Baptised by fire, the lad may well have felt nervous but he did it and did it well. Then he was sent over to the watercressbeds at Spettisbury to get more gravel. He did that five times that day, he says! Later on, he learnt to drive the firm's digger.

Earlier in the 'twenties, Archie Brennan had found a job at Sibley's Pottery over at Sandford. This involved him in a daily cycle ride, but that was no problem, nor was the fact that being the youngest employee he was always given the dirty jobs, like washing the clay. This he might have stuck at, but what infuriated him was the dirty tricks his fellow workers played on him, such as removing one of the links from his cycle chain, or taking the valve rubber out of his tyres. Both meant he had to walk home after work. Four months later his father heard of a vacancy at Churchill's nurseries. This was just off North Street, near to where the Health Centre is today and therefore much nearer to his home at Worget. He went off to apply but found another lad already there. Mr. Churchill gave both of them a task. The other boy was told to weed, but he set to pulling up everything! Archie had to return the following day and was give the tomatoes to see to. "I knew a little bit about tomatoes, so I got the job!" He was there eleven years, in spite of the fact that he had to work seven days a week from seven in the morning to five at night and that he was given no holiday at all during the period he worked there except for bank holidays.

Ray Herridge also found a job gardening, this time for Mrs. Pope up at Worgret Manor. He had already been going there for two years before he left school, working for her before and after his lessons. When he first applied she had explained to the twelve-year-old lad his duties as planting "two rows of potatoes, and plant as many marrows by the cesspit as you can," she said, "and in amongst other jobs you've got to clean the chicken houses out." Then she added that he could have "one of the cracked eggs each week. You are not to crack any of them to get an extra one, because I shall know." When he went there full time, he earnt 17s 6d (87 1/2p.)

For girls there was very very little, shop work or service. Doris Fooks managed to get taken on by Hicks', the town's department store in South Street, run by the

Blandford family who had expanded into neighbouring towns.

The frontage of their shop looks very much as it did in the 'thirties. They had acquired three places and had turned them into one large shop, with a single entrance. The door of what is now Bath Travel was then part of the window.

On entering the shop, the customer could turn left for the hosiery department, with stockings at 1/11 ¾ (nearly 20p). Doris remembered that staff could buy their stockings at the cost price of 1/6 (15p.). If it was material that the customer was after, then she came further into the shop, to what was always referred to as the Manchester Department. Nearby was haberdashery, but if she wanted her hair setting this was at the rear of the premises. Upstairs were the hats, dresses, jumpers and underwear. The wool department occupied what is now Bath Travel with a small staircase rising up to the first floor.

Doris Fooks at the back of "The Antelope" aged 16. Her father was very strict about the length of her dress, she did not dare to wear a shorter skirt. At the back of the Hotel her parents had tubs of flowers. [Doris James]

The Hicks sisters – Miss Gladys and Miss Eileen – took a lively interest in their Wareham branch and often slipped in to make a purchase and, no doubt, to cast a critical eye over the place. They came to Wareham for their stockings, or, at least, that is what they always seemed to buy, Doris recalled.

Staff at the shop numbered about ten or eleven under the control of a manager, a Mr. Whitlow during the Second World War years. Naturally the girls all had a uniform. Most Wareham shops closed for lunch at one o'clock, but Hicks' had sufficient staff to be able to keep open, with some assistants going for their lunch at twelve. During their break, the girls went up to the attic to eat and could sit on the ledge of the roof. They had a toilet outside at the back.

In addition to the shopworkers, there was also a sales rep, whose job it was to go round the area and bring back orders. Goods were then sent out on approval, a very popular feature of shopping then.

When she left school at 14, Joan Anderson found a job as an usherette in the Empire Cinema in West Street, carrying the chocolate tray up and down the aisles,

Symes Workers early 1920's in carnival mood. Standing: Annie White (Mrs Gover), Elizabeth Gover, ?, Thorne, –, Kit Dominey, –, –, Vernon Symes with his daughter, Mrs Symes, Miss Wootton, Miss Read and Miss Coombes. Behind: Rose Feltham (3rd from right) Front: Miss Balls, –, Benjafield, Miss Elmes and ?.
Francis V. Symes is listed in Directories 1911-1923 at 6 South Street. A Hicks is listed there 1931. [Author's Collection]

in her maroon coloured uniform with its cuffs, collars and its long sleeves. "Any noise and you'd flick on your pocket torch." The cinema was then owned by Cecil Elgar, who paid young Joan two shillings and six pence (12 1/2p.) a week. Out of this, she had to give her mother one shilling and six pence (7 1/2p.), leaving her with pocket money of one shilling (5p.). With this, she used to buy a pair of stockings in Woolworth's for six pence (2 1/2p.) and a threepenny (1 1/2p.) tin of Snow-Fire face powder, "and that was your pocket money!"

Marjorie Brewer had to go further afield, to Poole, where she found a job similar to Doris' at Bon Marche, also a department store. This one was in the High Street, about halfway between Poole Station and the Quay. Pay was even lower than that at Hicks', 5 shillings (25p.) a week, and out of this Marjorie paid 2/6 (12 1/2p.) for her train fare. Though she had no money to give her mother for her keep, it did get her out of the pub. "My father wanted me to help in the pub, but I wanted to get out and meet young people, not staying in the pub working with old men."

The shop opened at nine every weekday and did not close until six in the evening, with late nights on Fridays until seven and Saturdays until eight. Wednesdays, of course, like every other shop in the town, was half-day closing, at one o'clock.

Work in a shop involved long hours. Hicks opened at 9 o'clock every weekday and did not close until 6 in the evening. Bon Marche kept Marjorie there for another hour, till 7 o'clock Monday to Thursday. Both shops stayed open for an extra hour on Fridays and on a Saturday Doris finished at 8, while Marjorie stayed on until 9 o'clock.

"It was dark when I came back on the train –go up to the Poole Station. It always smelt of fish, or the gasworks, terrible! – get in a train. All the blinds were down. You'd open up a carriage door, grr!, the smoke! It was full of servicemen, all smoking! You couldn't see across the carriage room for smoke! Couldn't get a seat on the train. They were moving troops all over the place."

Hicks' Shop in South Street, about 1970. [Author's collection]

Bowles and Spencer's Bakehouse in Brixey's Lane, about 1970. [Author's collection]

Chapter 3
Shops and Services.

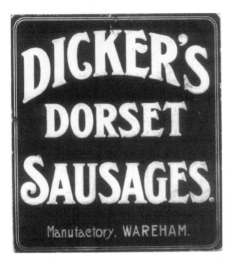

Until well after the Second World War Wareham was a town of small shops and so many Americans from the smaller towns would find this perfectly acceptable, but to their more sophisticated colleagues from the big industrialised cities Wareham shops must have seemed very old fashioned.

Many had changed little in the last fifty years, apart from some of the owners and were very similar to the ones described in *Wareham, Gateway To Purbeck;* for example, George Dicker's shops at 21 West Street and lower down the street were still there. He had taken over soon after 1881. His was a high class butcher's and grocer's. Its reputation was not just local for it supplied both the army camps at Lulworth and Bovington which Sammy Bye, who had married George's daughter, spent much time in fostering. Dicker's sausages were nationally famous.

The Spence girls used to be sent every Tuesday by their grandmother down to Dicker's asking, "Please, will you send a pound of sausages to Aunt Olive in Yorkshire?" Over half a century later their faces still reacted in ecstasy to the memory of those heavenly pork sausages! Their Aunt Maggie was another to whom they also had a pound sent.

Jack Tubbs used to go round to Cox's most days with a fourteen pound box or a twenty eight pound box of them all carefully packed. Cox was, among other things, agent for the Hants and Dorset Bus Company and sent the boxes to Williams and Treadgold's quality grocer's shop in Bournemouth Arcade, now Waterstone's Book Shop. Other boxes were sent up to Waterloo for the big London shops.

George Dicker used to employ four salesmen in the corner shop; Reg Farmer, Jerry Guy, Bert Stockley and Harry Meaden but no women, while he used to divide his own time between the accounts and serving customers.

In 1920 it was still a town of small independent shopkeepers. National businesses were only just beginning to find Wareham. As long ago as 1889 a branch of the

Co-op had opened. It is first mentioned in Kelly's Directories in that year. This was hardly an outside invasion as the next foreign firm did not come until 1915 when World Stores moved into 22 South Street, followed after the war by International Stores which acquired Marshallsay's important

Bennetts' shop in East Street [Ray Watkins]

grocery shop in 1920 (1 South Street). All three were therefore making inroads into what had been a local trade. The end of the war saw another invasion when, first of all, the big national giant, Frisby, opened shoe shops in both South and North Streets and, slightly later in the twenties, the Blandford Hicks family began taking over shops in South Street to turn into their department store. So gradually some of the town's trade was falling into the hands of outsiders. Whereas, in the past when outsiders acquired businesses they had moved into the town as residents,

Bennetts shop in East Street with its tiled floor. Ray Watkins had to sweep this every Monday morning, he hated it. [Author's collection]

32

these new owners did not. But even so by 1939 most shops were still in local hands.

Among the bakers it was the Bennett Brothers, who supplied, for the twenties and thirties, most of the locals' bread from their bakehouse in East Street. They also had their restaurant in North Street (now The Anglebury) and their grocery in front of the bakehouse in East Street. Established by their forebear Jonathan Bennett, before 1859, it was a very successful business. After being demobilised in 1920 Bert Grant was able to re-join this firm because he had worked there before he enlisted. Then he had been a delivery boy pushing the handcarts all round the town, out as far as Worgret in one direction, out to the station to the north and down to Bestwall and Swineham in the east, in all weathers, too! "If it was raining you put your macintosh on and put macintoshes over the goods," he later explained. If there was any spare time he washed and cleaned the tins and got the fruit ready for the bakers.

On his return in 1920 he found that old Phil Doll had left. He had been one of the important roundsmen before the war but his brother had died and he went back to take over his smallholding, Shepton Mallet way, so Bert was able to get his job. This was better than merely being an errand boy. At first with a horse and cart and later with a van he delivered, on different days of the week, to Sandford or to

Stoke or out to Ridge and Grange.

Harold tells his memory of Bert and his horse and cart stopping at the top end of Roper's Lane. There Bert would take out the number of loaves he wanted and set off down the lane, delivering them while the horse followed. When Bert had a van, he still stopped at the top of the lane, took out his loaves and set off delivering them. Harold can still picture the expression on Bert's face when he got down the end of the lane, glancing backwards as if expecting the van to be following.

Bert found it difficult to get used to the van as his son, David, related. "Dad had several spectacular crashes! He used to bring eggs back from the farms to the shop. He'd come back with the van full of eggs. This particular evening he failed to negotiate the

Bert Grant, taken in the 1950's
[David Grant]

33

bend at East Stoke. I don't think he'd been in the *Black Dog* but he ended up in the ditch! He eventually arrived home covered in eggs and blood!"

The other roundsman, Percy Best's brother, did all the town deliveries.

Bert was expected on a Sunday to give a hand with the furnaces. Bennetts had two steam ovens. Inside each were water pipes. When the oven heated up the water turned to steam. Bert said that steam was good for baking bread. Each oven had a window for the bakers to see how the bread was going. Both were fired by coke and they required constant stoking. His son David used to go with his father quite often when he was about six or seven. It was the smell of the burning coke that he remembered and all the waste that they used to burn, "Greasy paper had a smell of its own." On Saturdays the ovens were left to cool down, ready to be cleaned out on a Sunday morning. When this was done George Lucas was the one who usually re-lit the ovens, so the bakers could bake overnight which was for the shop or deliveries on the following morning. Flour was let down from the loft straight into the mixers. To help in the preparation there was a dough machine but Bert said "You had to turn a handle and it was hard work!"

Once mixed the dough was left to rise in big wooden troughs with wooden tops. It was upon them that the young David was sat . "I always remember sitting upon these and seeing rats. The place was ridden with rats — they were huge things – go scuttling by."

In addition to making bread the Bennetts also employed a confectioner. It was virtually a one-man-band. In the twenties this was George Lucas and later a Mr. Lee. He worked in a separate building preparing pastries, ordinary cakes and wedding cakes. There was an old gas stove here, an early type with five or six burners. If he wanted more heat Mr. Lee had a pile of sticks nearby and he would put these sticks on the gasburner.

When Bert went there before the joining up the confectioner had been Ern Bennett while Alf ran the bakehouse. Old Joe Bennett was in charge of the grocery shop. Bert recalled that on one occasion there was a great big argument going on in the bakehouse between the bakers about the furnaces. Mr Joe sent the girl who worked in the office out to "me and told me he wanted to see me.

'What do 'ee want?' I said.

'I don't know, but 'ee wants to see 'ee.'

When I went into his office, I said, 'Did you want to see me?'

He wrote out a note, and he said, 'You take this note out for Mr. Lock and Mr. Holt. On the note he had written, "Let brotherly love continue harmoniously together!"

Later, one of the employees left and set up on his own. Mr. Bowles found a premises not far away in Brixey's Lane and, with Mr. Spencer, he was able to use the skills he had acquired to produce bread of good quality that rivaled Bennetts.

Gover's sweet shop in North Street was a mecca for children and adults alike. In the thirties it was run by

On 18th August 1943, Dorothy and Phil sent this view of North Street to Mrs Browning of Dorchester. They were just about to visit their Auntie Doll who lived in a house on the right, near to the figures. Gover's sweetshop, the delight of children, is on the extreme left.
[Author's collection]

Gladdy Gover and her mother. They used to make home made sweets. Mint humbugs were their speciality. They cost about 2d (1p.) a quarter and were simply gorgeous, recalled Marjorie. "The shop was always filled with their distinct aroma when she was making them. It was a pokey little shop and yet she used to stay out in the little back kitchen and make these mint humbugs and they were lovely."

Another favorite haunt of children was Bussell's general shop which was further up North Street and which was crammed full with sweets. Mr. Bussell who kept the shop was an elderly man with a white moustache but it was his daughter, Cis, who in the thirties was serving the customers. *Kelly's Directory for 1939* gives his wife, Mrs E. Bussell, as proprietor. "I don't think Cis had much of a life really. She lived there and looked after her dad and ran the shop," recalled Marjorie, "When I used to get my Saturday penny (1/2p.) I used to go up there. All the sweets were in jars in those days. I used to say, 'I'll have a ha'penny's worth of those and a ha'penny worth of those!' As each variety was in a different jar and nothing was pre-weighed each quarter had to be weighed before it was sold. All this must have taken a lot of time."

Children also frequented another general shop in Church Street kept by two sisters, the Misses Knapp. Eddie Anderson confessed ashamed of his behaviour then, "When I was a lad, they looked about 120, but they must have been about 50 to 55. We used to get one Miss Knapp to go outside for a ha'peth (half a penny, but now only about ¼ of a penny) worth of gooseberries and get the

35

other one to climb up to the top shelves and, while she was looking, we'd fill our pockets up with the sweets they had on the counter. They survived and still made a living. That surprised me. We used to rob them blind."

Eddie also recollected that in the little area between Church Lane, Church Street and Davis Row, where he lived, "there were two grocers' shops. Next to one of the groceries was a family who used to sell eggs and a bloke around the corner used to sell wood and logs. One of his girls used to sell 'nickies' (bundles of small chopped pieces of wood). Then there was a chimney sweeper and a butcher. All these in this little group."

Butchers' shops were common in the town. Joseph Rose's was a long established butchery in West Street. In the early years of the century he had taken over from the Davis Family who had been there for most of the previous century. The Whittles were in South Street at no. 22, while next door were the Burgess Brothers at no 24. George Dicker also had a butcher's shop. Another long established shop was that of the Dugdales in North Street. When the first of the family is mentioned in the *Directories,* he was occupying no.13. By 1898 they had moved into no. 45 which is where older people still remember them. Between the wars it was run by two brothers, who always wore breeches and leather leggings. Wearing bowlers and stiff white collars was also a distinctive trait.

All the butchers still had their own slaughter houses. After all, ways of keeping meat fresh were still in their infancy so keeping animals alive until the last possible moment was the traditional way of trying to keep meat fresh. Dugdales' slaughterhouse was next to where the Post Office now is, around the corner in the lane. " I can remember," said Marjorie, "kids going down there on their way to school and seeing them slaughter the animals." Cows, sheep and pigs in the main streets were regular sights, as they were brought up to the slaughterhouses.

Dickers was behind the shops in West Street. About twenty to thirty pigs were slaughtered here each week. They were brought in mainly from Upton, and supplied by Hibbs, although whether he was the breeder, or merely the supplier, Jack Tubbs who used to work for Dicker as a teenager, did not know. The pigs arrived in the afternoon and were kept overnight. Good quality animals were always insisted upon. They usually weighed about ten stone but at Christmas smaller ones were in demand. They were killed with a humane killer. Once, they had a sow of about twenty-seven stone. The slaughterer, George Thomas, said, "It'll be alright," and he used the usual charge but the shot did not kill her. "There was a very long bench running down the side of the house and she got in under there. She sank to her knees, then suddenly got up! The bench flew up into the air! They got her again and shot her but it was still no good. They even partially cut her throat! In the end they shot her three more times before she was killed."

Usually animals were quickly slaughtered and hung up over night. The next day the carcasses were gutted and carved up, the joints being placed in a large walk-in fridge-freezer.

Not far from Dugdales in North Street was old Mr. Lucas's music shop. He was another man who always wore a bowler hat and had an old motorbike to get around tuning pianos and organs all round the area.

Another important shop in North Street was the ladies' high quality clothes shop, run by Mrs Ford. Her husband had bought 'The Yews', no. 7, in the middle twenties and had it modernised and converted by the local builders, Marsh. Mrs Ford was a milliner by trade and had served her apprenticeship in a large trading milliners in Bournemouth. The shop in Wareham did well as many of her clients came over from there. She used to hire rooms in the hotels to display her garments. Three ladies were employed to help in the shop. Her son Ken, as a lad, often helped with making the price tags. They all had to be made on the premises. He delighted, as boys would, in hanging a tag on the back of one shop ladies when she was not looking!

Elmes was one of the town's blacksmiths. It was an old established business. Years before it had been John Gillingham's (in the 1850s and 60s). Then big John Prince took it over. In his day locals tended to refer to Trinity Lane as 'Prince's Lane.' When he was demobbed from the army Herbie Elmes' dad bought it. Ray Herridge often used to go down and see him at work. "He used to let you blow the fire and I had to stand on a box to do it. I always used to get a bollocking because if you didn't blow it fast enough, or you blew it too quickly" the heat would be changeable, which did not suit the iron. Most of the trade was agricultural, and much of that involved shoeing. For shoeing a donkey the charge was 3 shillings (15p.), 5 shillings (25p.) for a pony and 8 shillings (40p.) for a horse. It did not matter how much the animal kicked and it took two men to shoe it, or whether it took the whole morning, the charge was always the same.

Young Herbie who started off working for his father did not care for the work. For one thing payment was not regular. Farmers often ran up too many bills and found it difficult to pay in the twenties. His father often used to complain that the last things farmers thought about was paying the blacksmith. One gentleman farmer, a Mr Bond, who lived at Worgret was very difficult to get any money from. A golfing, cricketing man, "dad shod his milk ponies, which he used to go round with the milk, and his carthorses. He owed about £80, which was a lot of money in those days. Father wasn't very business-like, a good worker, a craftsman, far too good. Mother was the businesswoman. Finally she wrote to Mr. Bond ,-

"Two years now, I've been sending bills in every two or three months. We haven't had any money .Wish you could see a way of settling up.'

He came down.

'Never get any blacksmith's bills! Gracious me, no! When you want it, just ask!

Here's a cheque.'

And it went on again for twelve months. He came down again and paid."

Ray Herridge also spent a lot of his time as a lad in the workshop of the town's other blacksmiths, the Newberys, two brothers.

Of course the market was flourishing and on Thursdays the whole town knew it. It was a much bigger event than it is today. Animals for the auction were still driven through the streets. Farmers came in with their wives to shop in their pony-and-traps, which could be seen with the horses, ponies and donkeys firmly tethered outside many of the pubs and hotels. In the thirties Effie Shaw came in from Sandford in her Morris car which at that time was very distinctive. There were so few cars around. Ray Herridge observed that "she always used to park on the pavement. Siddy Chilcott used to come out and lay into her. 'It's only partly on the pavement, Mr. Chilcott,' she used to say. Us children used to snigger."

Cattle and sheep were also there in plenty during Wareham Fair when lots of pens were set up by West Walls, on what is now the car-park. On market and fair days Eddie Anderson could earn a penny (1/2p.). "We used to tear out of school, go down the market and drive all the steers and cattle down to the station and put them on the train. We had to go in front and stop them going down the side lanes." David Grant has vivid memories of this. His family were still living in East Street then.

"They used to bring hundreds of cattle to the station by train and drive them through the streets up to the market. After they were sold they were driven back again. There was muck everywhere!"

Jack Tubbs' parents told him that on market days before he was born it was the custom for poor people who lived in Cow Lane to go down to the market with a pail and "they'd always came back with a pail of milk."

There was another market in the town then. Jeff's Market in Mill Lane was run, according to Ray Herridge, who would have been a boy at the time, "by a most weird lady. She had on one of those huge hats – like Queen Mary – a big flat hat with a dome on top. She seemed in charge." Jack Tubbs remembered it as selling more garden produce, with occasionally having chickens on its stalls. Its owners had a thriving business in Dorchester and this was a side line.

Gingerbread man often came to sell on market days and once Dora Spence saw a man making sticks of rock. "The first time he appeared at the Cross we couldn't understand how he did it. He just threw it over a hook and pulled."

With no washing machines and heavy linen sheets, shirts, and underwear, Mrs Earwaker's laundry service that she provided for the gentry was in great demand.

Started about the time of the Great War it had taken advantage of the great demand for laundry services at the camp during the war. "She was a good business woman, who could see the possibilities," commented Dora, her granddaughter. "For this increased demand her husband had built a proper laundry at the back of their house in Roper's Lane, No.15, and after the war there was plenty of demand from the local gentry, Alan and Leonard Sturdy at Trigon, Dr. Cunningham, Dr Snell, old Dr. Collihole and other doctors, farther afield such as Dr. Collier at Blandford. Then there were the Fillieuls at Sandford House, the Fords down at the garage below St. Martin's and the Clarks at Castle Combe, among her regular customers. The latter house was a great favourite with Mrs Earwaker's grandchildren, Jean and Dora, who loved "going up there. The cook would always have us in and give us a cup of cocoa and one of her home-made cakes!" said Jean. Her sister, Dora, added "and they did that down at Lacey's (at Bestwall)."

Their Uncle Bert collected all the soiled clothes on a Monday morning on his bike. Some houses had two hampers. The Sturdys, the Laceys and the Clarks, all did. Then the dirties were sorted and thrown into the copper which had been lit much earlier and the clothes boiled. In fact Bert and the other workers had spent most of a Sunday evening getting ready. Then while the clothes were boiling away three big tubs, placed long ways in a row, were got ready. Two women worked at one side of the three, two more opposite them and one more at either end. In the tubs the clothes were scrubbed and rubbed – all by hand.

There were as yet no washing powders so soap was bought in large bright yellow bars which had to be cut up into pieces. It had been put in a cupboard by the range to make it very hard.

The water for all this came from Grannie Earwaker's own well, "pure water; our drinking water; pumped up into the scullery." This water was used for most things but "a lot of fine washing, such as night gowns and fine lacy things, was all done in rain water from the butt. We had six or eight butts at the back of the house and they all ran into the laundry."

Most of the sheets were linen and were heavy when absolutely wet. They were put through the large box mangle. The box on the top had been filled "with concrete, concrete blocks, or stonemasons' blocks; and when you turned the handle the whole box went forward." The sheets were then put underneath the box on rollers; "great big wooden rollers." They were wound round onto one roller, with a spare roller next to it and another at the far end. As the handle was turned so the wet sheets "would go round the one and wound back onto the other one, so that all sides were being pressed." Jean commented with pride, "when they came out they were better ironed than what you can do today!"

After the blue rinse the other clothes were mangled. Uncle Bert usually did all the heavy work, the boiling, rinsing and mangling. If it was a wet day the wet clothes were hung over lines which stretched the whole length of the building and "with the big stove which was all hot and everything shut up the heat used to dry them. In about an hour it was dry enough to be pressed." (Jean)

This was the next big operation and it took a whole day but, before that, the tubs had to be cleaned out, scrubbed and packed up in the corner and the copper cleaned. — "it was a huge copper in the corner." (Dora). Then out came the ironing boards — "long and well padded. They brought them out and put them on a great big table." Everyone seems to have been involved in this. Uncle Bert, again, would do all the big things. "He was a marvellous ironer."(Jean). Their Grannie had a stove that was usually by the side of the copper but when it was needed it could be pushed out into the centre of the room. On the stove which was now red hot the irons would be placed in tiers. Grannie herself used to use the goffering iron for the lace frills down shirt fronts and on night gowns, pillowcases, maids' caps and aprons. It was a highly skilled job. "I can remember my grandmother just twisting the lace around her arm. She used to do it so quickly." Dora remarked, "as children, we all had our special little jobs." Jean used to get 2d (1p.) for ironing the handkerchiefs. "I used to love doing the handkerchiefs." Occasionally she would slip out and help turn the mangle. Dora said she did not mind using the goffering iron but "the only job I didn't like doing was the army socks! I hated socks!"

When the laundry was all done "everything used to look wonderful!" Then every item was packed into tissue paper, ready for Bert to deliver which he did on a Friday.

The girls also helped with the packages as well. "It was great for us kids to ride with a hamper on the handle bars! It was fun! Uncle Bert made a trolley which he fitted on the side of his bike but it was awkward to ride. He rode it alright."

The laundry was a full time job. Grannie Earwaker, the girls recalled, often worked well into the evenings to get everything ready for Fridays. It was full time for Uncle Bert and for the six women she employed. Mesdames Collier, Smith, Edwards, were some of the women whom her granddaughters could remember. "Mrs Gover came over a couple of times. Then there was Winnie Tollerfield." All were described by the girls as living "in the road," (Roper's Lane).

The Pure Drop in 1970, four years before it closed. In the 19th century this inn had several names, The Duke of York (1823-1842), The Carpenters' Arms (1842-1871) before becoming the Pure Drop in 1874. [Author's collection]

"The Yews" before it was altered by Mrs Ford to become her ladies' outfitters shop about 1931. 7 North street. [Author's collection]

Chapter 4
Leisure.

In that prehistoric age before television, computers, walkmans and the internet, what on earth did people do?

Basically, of course, they made their own amusement. There was nothing else. With virtually no cars in the back streets, boys, for example, could kick a ball without any worries and with family numbers still on the fairly large side, finding friends to join in presented no problems. Little Pitch and the Bowling Green were the two popular places in the town to find others to play.

"We'd go up round the Bowling Green and kick around there. Nothing organised," said Ray Watkins whose home, first in the Common Lodging House (69 North Street) and later in Elm Villas, meant that the Bowling Green was quite near him. Here the boys would kick anything. "No one could afford a football. We played with anything we could get hold of." Ray was very popular because he won a prize for perfect attendance at the Methodist Sunday School. The prize was a football. "I was only small then and I wasn't old enough to take over. I used to take my ball up and the big lads used to join in. All of the lads were older and bigger than me. They used to use it more than I did. When the ball got a puncture, there was always a dad who found a new bladder or a new lace."

When they felt they had mastered basic skills, they might, like Harry Rawles, Vic Lillington and Ray, perhaps get chosen to play for one of the town's teams –the Minors, the Juniors or the Seniors. The latter was made up of those who were best at football, for they played in the South Dorset League Division 1, against towns in the county. The Juniors, those who were not quite good enough for the Seniors, were in Division 2 and the Minors, those who were not as good as the Juniors, played in

Wareham Football Club 1922. Back: Henstridge, T. Perry, J. Guy, R. Lane. Middle: C. Yea, Percy Tewkesbury, H. Best. Front: F. Wensit, ?, E. Stockley, W. Ferry, ? [Author's collection]

Division 3. These two divisions were zoned. "We were in the area with Longfleet (Poole). It did not matter about age. You could be as old as you wanted, men and boys as soon as they were old enough. After the Second World War, Beasley was only fifteen when he played for the Seniors."

All the teams were selected by a committee of about twenty which, at least after the Second World War, used to meet at the *Pure Drop* in West Street on a Monday night. "It used to take them hours. We used to go up and wait outside. Officially we weren't allowed to drink."

Keen players, of course, wanted to get picked for the Seniors. "I remember once," recalled Ray, "I was in the Seniors' Cup and they had to play Poole Town and they went down. I went to watch. The goalkeeper never turned up for our team, so they came round and collared me. 'I'm not playing down there,' I said.

'Yes! You are!' they said.

So I played for the Seniors' Cup. We lost. There was no protection for goalkeepers then. They were big lads, and I was about 15 or 16. They were Seniors."

All boys used to play in ordinary hob-nailed boots. Special boots were far too expensive. "We used to kick each other," said Harold, "but it was all good fun. The worst team we ever played was out at Morden, and they were farmers' sons. We always knew we were going to get a hiding there. They were a rough lot." The Workhouse lads were also to be feared. Their boots were heavier and more studded. A kick from one of them could be very painful.

For boys there was also the Monday Club, where under instruction they learned the skills of boxing. It was held down at Wareham Market. Harold went ."We had an instructor. He used to say, 'Come on! Hit me!' and I did. I hit him and knocked him down, and he nearly went for me. I had to defend myself. I thought, no more of this for me!" Harold never went back although others stuck to it.

However, children found plenty to do. For David Grant, Youth Club could take up several evenings. Then two nights were spent on choir practice and on Sunday evenings he was singing in the choir. Thus, he did not find he was bored.

Ray Herridge too, enjoyed chapel life. "We used to go to a lantern slide show, with a bun and a cup of cocoa, in a little shed that used to be something to do with keeping cattle in for Skinny Whittle, the butcher. Here we learned gospel choruses, like *I'm H.A.P.P.Y* and *Wide Wide As The Ocean."*

For Dan'l Coombes, apart from football, it was the Town Band that he got involved in, joining in 1942 at the age of thirteen. "It was winter," he recently recalled, "and we were walking the streets, a gang of us, eleven, twelve and thirteen

WAREHAM TOWN BAND
NATIONAL BAND FESTIVAL, ALEXANDRA PALACE
1937

Back: third from left, White. Middle: left Frank Gover (Nocky) 3rd from right Len Gover. Front: 2nd from left George Gover (Band Master), 3rd from left Wilt Stich. [Author's collection]

year olds, just walking up and down the town in the dark. What could we do? All of a sudden this bloke came along and said;

> 'I could do with all you boys,' he said, 'Are you interested in music? … Well?…why don't you come up. I'll arrange to see the schoolmaster and we'll borrow the school room for the evening."

And that is how Dan'l and his friends found themselves in the Town Band, but it did not prove to be quite what they thought, as Dan'l explained; "It was so boring. It was unbelievable, yet we took to it. It was something to do in the evenings; twice a week. We started with blackboard scales and how to read music. We started going on Sunday mornings."

Of course, most of the local men who had formed the band had been called up into the services, but all their instruments were still in the Town Hall, and when the bandsman felt the lads were ready, they went down to the Hall to select their instruments. That was a "very great day!" says Dan'l, and no doubt many an excited lad rushed eagerly home to show parents. Dan'l's dad was not at all pleased!

"My dad said, 'You can get out in the fields with that noise!'

So I practised in the air raid shelter! It was at the top of the garden! I used to go

Dan'l Coombes loved to escape from the town and go to Slepe, where his granparents lived. This picture taken in 1936 [Dan'l Coombes]

up there and practise Baritone, Euphonium and Bell trombone."

Harry White was the bandsman, with George Gover who trained the boys. Old Mr. White was very strict but George knew how to handle us boys. We would never have stuck it with old Mr. White."

Typical of children of this period were the Andersons of Davis Row. Joan recalled, "As children we used to play in the cemetery at night. We were not frightened. There was no evil there. We played Hide and Seek among the tombs, and no one complained (about us being there)." Her brother, Eddie, said much the same; "We thought nothing of it!" Joan continued, "Everyone in the area used to play there, until their mums called 'Time to come in!" That, Joan said was about 7 o'clock. Eddie added, "perhaps a little later, eight or nine o'clock at night." Joan went on, "the policeman used to walk round to see what was going on, and if we saw him coming we used to lie down under the wall and keep very quiet, and he'd walk on by and say; 'It's alright! I know you're there!'"

From the chestnut tree in the area they used to get conkers, and in the road they played cricket. The wicket was drawn on the cemetery wall. "We stood one side of the road and played the other."(Joan)

For the lads around Edward's Crescent, Nundico and the north end of the town, summer days were largely spent on the North River. It was an endless source of pleasure. Harry Rawles spent most of his spare time down there. At Sandpit on the North River he learned to swim when the bigger boys picked him up and threw him in the water! It was a case of learning very quickly! Even so, for all the children who used to go

Harold and Ray spent many a happy hour down by the river with their friends, as did countless boys throughout the centuries. [Author's collection]

up there, Ray Watkins recalled, no one was ever lost in the river. Here they swam, fished, played Cowboys and Indians and had a good time. Sometimes, their help was appreciated by older men laying fishing nets across the river near the gasworks. When the tide turned, the children helped them pull in the nets. Twenty to thirty mullet might be caught in this way. After the war, all fishing in the river was stopped.

On other occasions the lads used to cut down reeds just above the trap hatches upstream of Baggs' Mills, bind them together and then throw them in the water, making rafts of the great heaps. Then they would jump on these rafts in spite of the reeds being all covered in leeches! They would let the current bring them downstream till the rafts fell apart. Usually they could get down to Rolling Bay, by North Mills, before this happened. "It was great fun!" Harry recalls.

Ray Watkins also spent many a happy hour up river of the mill, two to three hundred yards up towards the Common, where there was a big sandpit and the water here was not deep, only paddling depth.

"I'm going up river today, mum," he would announce.

"I don't like you going up river," his mum would answer.

She would always let him go, but not without a couple of sandwiches and a bottle of pop. Off he would set in an old pair of khaki shorts and a pair of sandshoes, and a little old shirt, that "used to last us all summer." There he would stay until the end of the day. "Mother had to come up and fetch me. She knew there were older children that could look after us, so we'd never come to any harm."

The watermeadows below the walls where children have played through the ages. [Author's collection]

Nor, it seems, did any harm come to Harold and his friends when they took old tyres up Roper's Lane and up to the top of the Walls there. A lad would curl up inside a tyre, someone would then give it a push that sent the tyre rolling quickly down the slope and into the lane; "great fun," Harold commented!

Another place they often went was over to Carey Woods. They would buy a pennyworth of stale cakes (yesterday's) and off they would go to play at camping.

But life was changing. The inter-war years saw the spread of radio in Britain. Herbie Elmes made his own sets, simple crystal ones for his friends, and no doubt there were others in the town who did the same. Percy Westerman, the "Gung-ho" writer of adventure stories, lived on a houseboat on the river below the town. He was regarded as an authority on such sets, having been a wireless officer in the navy, and he was a familiar sight in the town dressed in a kind of naval uniform. Young Herbie would often run along the towpath to see him and get his advice. These sets, very primitive by modern standards, seemed magical to people at the time, hearing music and voices seemingly conjured up out of the air! For Ray Herridge and his friends, it was a special treat to be able to gather round the living room table and hear music coming out of the set, which had to be stood in a mixing bowl to make the faint sounds louder. For Harry, it was an exciting art to wriggle the cat's whisker to pick up the sounds and try to get them louder without losing them.

Later on, valve sets came in, and Ray used to go to Jack Strange's cottage in North Street, where the haircutter had a very large up-to-date set. There they would listen to *In Town Tonight*, a popular radio chat show of the thirties and forties. Harold recalled when his father bought their first real radio – a Cossar – about three feet high it stood. Sometimes, it did not work. "I remember once dad threw a knife at it to make it go!" Sets like this ran off batteries and accumulators. The latter had to be recharged every so often, and Harold seemed forever to be running down to Cleeve's garage. This was a typical thing for garages to do at this time; not that it brought in that much income. Cleeve's were typical in charging 6d (2 1/2p) for this service. If they were too busy to do it, Harold would go off to Churchill's in East Street, or to Burt's, in West Street. As with most sets, the Rawles's one could only get two programmes, the Home Service (now radio 4) and the Light programme(now radio 2), together with a great deal of crackling! A similar radio stood in the Grants' home in about 1934. They bought it from Cyril Cottee, who came down and put up the aerial for them. *The Cloister and the Hearth* was one programme that made a deep impression on young David, especially on dark evenings with only the light from the fire.

Between the wars was the age of the bicycle. The Rawles Family used to cycle a lot, especially down to Shipstal, beyond Arne, to have a swim. When they were very young, Harry went on his mother's bike, while his sister rode on her father's bike. Once when they were going there, "I was only eight or nine, and my foot slipped off the frame and went in the front wheel as we were going down a hill. It brought us all off our bikes and ended cycle rides for good! I was more concerned about not being able to get to Shipstal."

For young adults, dances were all the rage, especially those held in either the Drill Hall in North Street or in the Corn Exchange. Both were very popular, though the former, the Drill Hall, was preferred.

"It had a lovely floor," recalled Marjorie Jeffries. "Dances were held there years before the war. There was the Flannel Dance, where the men wore grey flannels…. the Daffodil Dance, where every lady had a bunch of daffodils. When it was interval time, the *King's Arms* used to get packed out, it was just cross the road. They could only serve teas and coffee as refreshments in the hall. Coach loads of troops from Bovington Camp used to come for a dance before the war. They used to dash over for a drink." When Marjorie went dancing her father was always just by the door to walk her home, even though it was just across the road. When the dance hall was bombed, the only place they could have a dance was the Town Hall, so that was used.

Some girls, like Doris Fooks, even went farther afield to dances. Bovington Camp was a popular venue.

The years between the wars saw the heyday of the cinema. Wareham's was an old one, or at least by the thirties it was well established. In 1900, 'animated photographs' had been shown at the Oddfellows' Hall as part of the popular entertainment programmes that were put on there. Gradually 'moving pictures' became more frequent, especially with the closing of the army camp up the Worgret Road after the First World War. In the interwar years, the cinema was run by Mr. Merrick.

It was very popular, with long queues developing for the films that everyone wanted to see. Ray Herridge was lured there. His ladies were very religious and did not go to the pictures, but he "did a bunk off after choir and went and saw *The Phantom Of The Opera.*" After that, he used to go regularly, earning 3d.(1p.) as a delivery boy for the Wool Shop. That got him into the pictures, leaving him 1d(1/2p) for a bag of broken biscuits.

Not that the audience were that quiet

Once known as The Empire, the cinema was extremely popular, with long queues most nights. [Author's collection]

48

and receptive. Some could be little horrors, as Ray recalled; "We used to throw things at Mrs. Merrick in the picture house, when we were there. They used to threaten to stop the film... throw things at the screen and make holes in it ... little buggers we were. Mr. Merrick occasionally came out and shouted at us, but not so much."

Later, after the war, Mr Merrick was killed in an aeroplane accident, and his wife took over the running of the cinema. "His death made a great impression on the town."(Ray)

Some went farther afield to the cinema, in Poole. One who did was Grannie Earwaker. "The highlight was going every other week into Poole," explained her granddaughter, Jean. "We used to go to Hawkes' shoe shop in the High Street every other Saturday. Very friendly with old Mr. Hawkes ... a taxi from the station ... marvellous! ...down Poole High Street. Everyone from the Road (Roper's Lane, and around there) used to ask my grandmother to bring shoes back for them. She'd pay for them, and they'd pay her back so much a week. We'd come back with boxes of shoes!.

Then, we'd go to the Regent at Poole to see a picture, if it was a picture my grandmother wanted to see!" Her sister, Dora, added, "Al Jolson and *The Singing Fool* and *The Count of Monte Cristo* we saw three times! She (Grannie) was mad on *Disraeli*. She loved that!"

Other things that were very popular were the Empire Day festivities, George V's Silver Jubilee celebrations of 1935 and the annual Wareham Carnival.

In the thirties and the years after the War, no Wareham carnival was right if the Muddlecombe Men were not there! They were a band of locals who started in 1933 when Gordon Sansom, the landlord of the *New Inn*, now the *Quay Inn*, had the idea of creating a bit of fun around the town's old fire engine. Ted Brennan, Frankie Edwards, Sid Lumber, Herbie Elmes and Gordon came up with the Muddlecombe Fire Brigade (photo p.81). Not only did it gain first prize at Wareham, but entered into similar carnivals at Poole and Boscombe, it won the top award in each.

1934, the lads devised the Muddlecombe Laundry. "A trail of soap suds marked the course of the Carnival parade through the town, and this unusual evidence of passing gaiety was provided by the hard-working 'Muddlecombe Laundry' tableau. That exceedingly humorous turnout, the work of Mr G. Sansom and friends, which has already taken first prizes at Poole, Boscombe and Swanage Carnivals, again carried off the premier award for tableaux." (The *Daily Echo*)

Herbie always reckoned that Sandie Powell, the great star of radio and variety, who during the Second World War brought his listeners regular news about

Muddlecombe, probably saw the Wareham men's float at Boscombe Carnival and was intrigued by the name.

In the photo, outside the *New Inn*, George Cox is seen with his horse, Diamond, and his cart. Behind are Ted Brennan, Frankie Edwards, Sid Lumber, Gordon Sansom and Herbie Elmes, all dressed as washer women. [photo: Herbie Elmes]

And then there were the pubs. Wareham had a lot more pubs than it does today, although there were not as many as there had been sixty years before. The pub was a social centre, a leisure centre, somewhere for men especially to go in the evenings and enjoy themselves. "When I first started drinking," in the late thirties, recalled Dora Spence, "I'd say I was going down Yorkie's, not down the *Duke of Wellington,* and I used to go to Ma Fooks's, not to the *Antelope.*"

The Brewers were the landlords of the *King's Arms* in North Street. They came there in 1933, after Ted Brewer had been made redundant as a driver by BP. The manager of the Poole depot suggested that he take a pub and gave him a good reference. Strongs of Romsey, the brewers, accepted him and offered the *King's Arms.* It took a lot to get used to the idea, for Ted and his wife were not 'drinkers,' but they made a good go of it and stayed until they retired in 1968.

The *King's Arms* had flagstone floors, a pokey little kitchen and no bar counter, which made life difficult for the landlord. Every drop of beer and spirits had to be brought up each time from the cellar. This meant endless trips down the stairs and back again. Things were easier in this respect at the *Antelope* in West Street

Celebrating Empire day 1922

Back Row: Stickland, Stickland, Harry Selby, Bert Speed, John Randall, Kruger Hodge, Walker from the station and Sid Fry Middle Row: Kanga Welstead, ? Front Row: ?, Pip Arthur Boyce, George Welstead, Sid Norris, Benny Lucan, Alfie Shears.

Silver Jubilee Celebrations, 6th May 1935

Percy Best's daughter, Jean, and son, Brian, in the centre.

Waiting for the procession, May 12th 1937

[All, Author's collection]

Dressed up for the Jubilee, 6th May 1935. Joan Skinner, Ray Dean, Cath Toop and Ray Watkins in front. [Ray Watkins]

Wareham Carnival in 1930s.
Above: The mayor's car leading the procession. The next float is "The Salmon" constructed by Mr Cox, the fishmonger in South Street.

Left: A float with the inscription "Oranges and Lemons say the Bells of St. Clements. [Both: Author's collection]

where William Fooks was in charge. It too had a stone flag floor in the bar, which his daughter Doris, as a schoolgirl had to scrub, but it did have a bar counter.

The average price for a pint just before the Second World War was 4d (2p.), and five Woodbine cigarettes (a cheap popular brand at the time) cost 2d (1p.). At this time cigarettes were mainly sold loose, rather than in packets.

Regulars had their own corner. At the *King's Arms,* Harry Farwell, Old Mr. Strange and George Humble were often in. They enjoyed a good joke and were always pulling one another's leg. They were great gardeners, and spent many hours in the pub comparing the size of their allotment-grown vegetables, each trying to outdo the others.

The "Kings Arms" in North Street, 2002 [Author]

Although most of their customers were men, there were some old ladies who slipped in. Such ones were Mrs Hodge and her next door neighbour, Mrs Stevens. They lived in a row of cottages on East Walls, which were rather tumbledown, but they did bring up their families there. They came in the mornings, about 11 o'clock. Mrs Hodge had her glass of stout, while her neighbour enjoyed her half of bitter. That would cost her 3 1/2d (1 1/2p.) While they drank, they would get very excited picking out the horses and have 3d (1 1/2p.) each way. "They always used to enjoy themselves." (Marjorie)

Old Mrs Christopher was another regular up North Street. A little bent old lady dressed in black skirts and black boots, she used to bring her black bag with her, and take back six pints of draught bitter to do her washing with. "Washing day today," she would say, "so I must have one (a drink) while washing." "That," observed Marjorie, "is what kept her going."

It was Marjorie's job to run up to Mrs Gerrard's on a Sunday morning to fetch the old lady's bag fill it with six pints of beer and take it back. "Sometimes she used to say 'Bring down a miniature whiskey.' That was her's. 'Don't let the old man see it, mind!' She used to moan about him. He'd go down the *Duke of Wellington's* for his drink. She'd make him sleep in the attic when he came home drunk, but she'd have her little tipple."

Alfie Gerrad was an old soldier from the First World War. "We always knew when he used to go to the Reunions. I used to be up in bed, and he'd come rolling up the road at 12 o'clock, singing 'Comrades, Comrades!"

Over at the *Pure Drop*, some of the regulars were highly colourful characters. After the war, when Jack Tubbs kept the pub in West Street, a frequent visitor there was an old chap who had survived the *Titanic*. Jack remembered him as a dapper little chap, who never used a safety razor. He claimed he had been a shepherd and regularly drove his sheep up to Westminster!

Sid Thompson was another regular at Jack's pub. An old seaman, described as a very scruffy chap, he used to live for his beer and be at the pub drinking all the morning. "He'd go in the pub until lunchtime. As soon as they were thrown out, he'd go along to Georgie Dicker's. There he'd get a couple of pig's trotters, go up on the Walls and eat them, and throw the bones anywhere. Then he'd have a kip, until the pubs opened again, and then he'd go back in."

Jack also recalled "an old ploughman who used to live up the almshouses, a real character, who used to toddle down to the *Pure Drop* … in his 80s … used to plough with a horse team. He'd come in and have his two pints … then wander off and come back for another. One day he came in.

'Pint, Bish?'

'Please, Mister.'

He put down his shilling(5p.) and ha'penny.

'I'll have to owe you a ha'penny!'

'That's alright, Bish. Forget all about it."

The following day when he came in for his pint, he put down a ha'penny.

'Lookee, Mister. That ha'penny!'

And he insisted I took it, or 'I'll not come in 'ere again!'"

Though all of these three memories date from after the war, the three men must have been around the town for many years before, and probably frequenting the *Pure Drop*.

Eddie Anderson talked about other 'characters' he knew as a young man. Sam Jordan was one. He used to work at the Pottery at Sandford. "He didn't like going fast on his bike, so he used to walk down any hills," and, as the journey from the town out to the Pottery involved two hills, "he used to push his bike from Wareham to Sandford in the mornings and push his bike back again at nights. He did it regularly."

Siddy Coates was always catching moles and making them up into moleskin trousers. If anyone in the area caught a mole, he saved it for Siddy. Walt Watts,

The Antelope was a Hotel, not just a pub [Doris James]

'Action' Watts, could often be seen down on the Common with his gun. Jesse Green spent his time down on the river, or trying to sell watercress around the streets. Jack Hodge was often down on the other river.

These were, in Eddie's view, proper characters about the town, often loners during the day, but at night, "all intermingled at the pubs."

In spite of some rather scruffy characters, pubs attracted whole families. The Orchards, the Frys, the Marshallsays, all came to the *King's Arms*. At Christmas, their numbers were expanded with aunties and uncles and grandparents. "They all came together for a good evening out."

Bank Holidays were especially busy. No one had a car, instead people went out to the pub for "a glass of beer, a chat and a sing-song. They'd get out in the backyard, and someone'd bring an accordion out and they'd sing. They'd put some sand down, and old Bill Skinner used to do the sand-dance, until his mother'd call;

    'Come on home, Bill.'

    'Alright, mother, I'm coming!'"

Over at the *Antelope*, it was the same. Everyone loved a singsong. "Someone played the piano," recalled Doris, the landlord's daughter there. Sometimes, she used to play.

Then there were the pub outings, which were great social occasions. Marjorie's mother was in charge of the arrangements at the *King's Arms*. "We used to go to the Isle of Wight, sometimes to Southsea. There were youngsters. The youngsters and the old folk would mingle together on a coach. Take some beer on board,

The landlord of the Antelope, Bill Fooks, and his wife, Edith, in her musquash coat, the height of fashion. [Doris James]

and mother would pack up hundreds of sandwiches and crisps and all that. They would pay for it, so much a week. They had a wonderful time!"

Different publicans in the town had their favourite places to go. The *Horse and Groom* regulars always went to the racecourses, at Cheltenham, for example.

In an age before free national health, pubs ran slate clubs for their customers, who paid 6d a week. If a member fell sick, he would receive 10 shillings a week (50p.), but he would have to be in by 9.30pm each evening.

A Thrift Club was run for Christmas, and this was used to pay for extra beer. On Thrift Club Night, the Brewers always had a big party. "Mother used to do up sandwiches and buy the beer. They always had to get a piano player in, and they had a wonderful sing-song. I remember being up in bed and hearing them sing away. Each man had his own song. Harry Fallows always used to sing *The Laughing Policeman;* Mr. Fred Brown *What Ho! She Bumps,* and my uncle sang about a cockledoddledo! When war came, we'd get the troops in, and there was always some member of the troops who could play. Then we would have some good nights!" (Marjorie)

Yorkie Yates and his wife Dulcie at *The Duke of Wellington* were great characters. He had once been a jockey, and, not surprisingly, he was not very tall, an "apple dumpling of a man." (Marjorie) Dulcie was a lovely person, blessed with a great laugh.

"When she was laughing at the *Wellington*, you could hear her on the Cross!" In spite of being a publican's wife and in the bar, she would not touch alcohol! She always drank water. She used to love dancing. Later, when there were LDV evenings at the *Grosvenor*, she and Yorkie used to dance and although she was a big lady, she was as light as a feather on her feet.

Don Charles kept the *Black Bear* during the thirties. A bit of a dandy, Marjorie recalled him as wearing Plus-fours.

There were more visitors to the town in the thirties. It was a period when nationally people had more free time and many were taking the opportunity to get out into the country. Cycling was popular, not only with the locals, but with people coming from Poole and Bournemouth first by train and then taking their cycle from the guard's van, they were free to roam the roads and lanes of the Purbecks.

This affected Wareham in two ways. More cafes opened to cater for thirsty visitors, and more places took in overnight guests. The *Antelope* was one of the pubs that did bed and breakfast. "People came from all over the place," recalled Doris Fooks. The guests' rooms were on the first floor, where there was a bathroom

The Lord Nelson where Maurie Ash reigned as landlord. This view taken in late 1960s. [Author]

and toilets. (This was long before the days of every guest room having an *en-suite*). The *King's Arms* also did bed-and-breakfast.

Maurie Ash was another who took in visitors. This was something which Maurie and his wife started at *The Lord Nelson*. They had not been in the pub two or three weeks when they were asked by a schoolmaster and his son to put them up.

"We don't do any Bed and breakfast," Maurie told them. "We've got beds up there ready to start, but we haven't carpeted the place or done anything. We've only been in a fortnight."

"We don't mind, so long as there's a bed!"

So that was the start of their taking in visitors. The schoolmaster and his son must have enjoyed their stay, for they came back, Maurie recorded, for the next four or five years.

Other guests also came back year after year. One family used to come from Coventry. First they came as singles, then as a married couple, and then with their children.

Maurie never advertised, but the *Nelson* seemed always to be full. One mother and her baby daughter came to stay. They had a double room and the uncle who came with her hired a single. In the morning, it was clear that only the baby had slept in the double bed. Her imprint was clear. "You ought to have seen the single bed! Didn't even straighten the bedclothes to camouflage anything!"

Another set of people Maurie remembered well were four, "really nice people. They had a drink and went upstairs on the last evening" of their stay. The next morning when he took the tray of tea in, he quickly went back downstairs to his wife.

"They've changed partners! In the front room, one lady sat up and took the tray, and I'd just go in and pull the curtains back and say, 'It's a nice day. You're going to enjoy yourselves today,' or something like that. Goes off to the other. Tap the door. Say 'Good morning' The one there I used to put on the little table. They never moved.

When I went in there that morning. I was surprised. She did take the tray! I realised it was the party from the other room! It caught me unawares!"

Another visitor turned out to be a millionaire, who came to the *Nelson* when the *Black Bear* was full. He seemed to enjoy it just having Bed and Breakfast, for he came back several times. Once he remarked to his host, "I envy you, Mr. Ash. 'Tisn't money. I've got plenty of that. I'm a millionaire. I come down to you because no one knows where I am!"

In addition to the guests, coach parties came. The coaches parked outside, which with the traffic today seems very surprising.

An additional attraction at the *Nelson,* was a tame fox that had been brought in as a young cub and the family had taken pity on him and looked after him. When he got a bit older, it was the landlord's youngest daughter, Peggy, who took charge, taking him on a lead for walks round the Walls, and bringing him into the bar to entertain the customers. The fox, Maurie said, always knew when it was closing time! "He'd start sharply barking! When the crowds had gone, he'd be let out into the bar and he'd pick up the bits dropped, especially the crisps. He loved crisps."

One question that many of Maurie's visitors asked was whether Lord Nelson did actually stay in the building. Maurie's standard answer was; "We don't advertise it, because Lady Hamilton stayed with him!"

A very popular activity in the interwar years - hiring a char-a-banc to explore. Here Percy Best and his wife are at Gough's Cave, Cheddar. [Author's collection]

Section 2 - A TOWN UNDER SEIGE.

Chapter 5

Wareham Prepares

When the Yanks arrived in Wareham during 1943, Britain had already been at war for over four years, something which some Americans were inclined to forget. A group of them stationed at Organford once asked the teenage Bob Thompson where the local Englishmen were as they had not seen any young men around. He had to remind the newcomers that most of them were away fighting and had been for the past few years.

Bill Sergeant in charge of Wareham Waterworks, probably with his son, Freddie. [Author's collection]

To put a country on a wartime footing was a mammoth task, and one which the government had started a year before 1939, at the time of the Munich Crisis, but little was really achieved until after the Nazi invasion of Poland a year later. Fortunately, for Britain, the declaration of war was not followed by a German air bombardment of London pounding the country into surrender, which they had done to Poland. Instead, they left Britain alone, and this became known as "The Phoney War." This gave the British government time to get the country ready for war.

Obviously, shelters were a priority for the civilian population, for the coming war would initially be from the air, so all over the country, shelters were made. Under advice from the government, Wareham Town Council, in May 1939, had a demonstration trench dug up at Westport House for townsfolk to see and, hopefully, go home and dig one in their back gardens. During the same month, the local police applied for permission to place a warning siren on the Town Hall.

Later, when war was declared, the Town Crier was sent round the streets calling everyone out to help dig trenches for the local schools. Edie Joyce's father went and helped at Stoborough School. *The Dorset County Chronicle* on 14th September

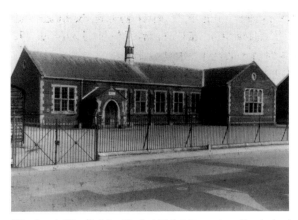

Wareham's Church School built 1885-6. It was an all age school until the Senior School was built in 1939. [Author's collection]

reported that this work was well in hand at the Church School, at the Senior School, and over at Sandford School.

Wareham had just built this Senior School. It should have been ready for the September intake. Ray Watkins was one of the new boys. Only the school was behind schedule, so he and all the other pupils were given another three weeks holiday. When they did go back, the new school had been provided with shelters. These consisted of six foot deep trenches dug zigzagging across the field at the very far end, very close to the Commons' boundary. The sides of the trenches were then shored up with galvanised metal sheets. More sheets were put on top to form a roof. Earth was then heaped on the top of these, making a mound two or three feet thick, which soon became grassed over. Ray does not think they would have survived a direct hit, but they did protect from shrapnel.

"Our first raid was a disaster!" confessed Ray Watkins recently. "It was planned to evacuate the school orderly. Everyone was expected to go with his class and follow his leaders. But the siren went, and everyone just flew … all the kids running across the open field; all hell … mayhem! Just after the all-clear went, we all came back again and saw many of the children lying flat on their backs. Everyone started saying, 'They're dead!' They were motionless. Fortunately, we found they had just fainted with excitement. The teachers were outside trying to get them back."

Ray Herridge was still at the Church School. The trenches for them were on the Bowling Green, but later on further trenches were built in the school gardens. At first, he remembered, these did not have roofs. They came later.

There was, of course, no lighting inside the shelters. To overcome this, one boy or girl in each class at the Senior School was put in charge of the hurricane lamp for his/her class. Because he was a good sprinter, Harold Rawles had this job for his class. If the siren went he had to pick up the lamp and run across the school field to the shelter to be there before the rest of the class arrived. Everyone had to go, not straight across the field, but round as near the hedge as they could. When they reached the shelters, the boys went in one end and the girls at the other, and they would meet in the middle. The lamps in that area would get blown out. "It was all good fun! Everyone treated it as a joke."(Ron)

The shelters "had a damp smell, a cellar smell", said David Grant. "The paraffin lamps had their own smell….. Even with the lamps, it was still pretty dark down inside." The lamps did not give out much light.

Inside the shelters, there were wooden slatted benches running down each side to sit on and duckboards on the floor to walk on, rather than the bare wet earth. Their teachers were there, but they did not sit with their classes. Instead, they would come along with a torch periodically to see they were alright, but otherwise there was nothing to do. The children just sat there and talked. David recalled; "Sometimes we were there for hours on end."

"We got browned off," remarked Ray Watkins. No wonder he considered 1939/40 "a wasted year. We spent it running backwards and forwards to the shelters… The siren went regularly about two o'clock, and the 'all-clear' wouldn't go till a quarter past three. At first, the teachers would not let you go out of the shelters, even though the 'all–clear' had gone, Then some of the mums used to come and collect their children. Those who were still there at the end of the school were sent home, if there were no planes about. (Later) we used to come out and just sit on the grass until it was time to go home."

In between being in the shelters, Harold recalled spending some of his school time going up to Worgret to get sand. "It was one of our jobs" The sand was used to fill bags. These sandbags were for protecting buildings in the town, like the Town Hall.

Many locals built their own shelters. Dan'l Coombes' father constructed his in the back garden, using concrete. Not only did it have steps going down into it, but it even had the luxury of electric lights! During the warning siren, some of his neighbours came in. Over at Elm Villas, Mr. Stretch, who lived at no.6, got all the men from the villas, including Ray Watkin's father, to dig out a shelter. "He was in the

Dug Out at Wareham Water Works. [Author's collection]

building trade. They dug into the steep bank in front of the houses, and made the shelter. It was a good one, with reinforced concrete and earth on top. It would have taken a good old bit to shift it."(Ray)

Not everyone had a shelter. It was felt that the innkeeper and his family at the *King's Arms* would be safe using the pub cellars, and Phyl Marsh and her mother had their own cellar under the old farmhouse out at Arne. In fact, few outside the town had a shelter. Doris Samways, out at Carey, did not. Her family stayed inside the house during a raid.

Beryl Binding's family in their fairly new council house at Nundico, of course, did not have a cellar. If there was a raid, they had to hide under the stairs. She remembered very well one occasion when they didn't. They all dived under the kitchen table. That was the night they lit the decoy at Arne, and the whole area seemed to go up in a blaze.

"You could hear the bombs whistling down. We all dived under the table, with our legs out. What good would it have done? My sister said, 'I want a drink of water!' Everytime someone went to get her a glass of water the bombs'd come down again. We really thought Wareham would be flattened.

The chap next door said; 'Can my mother come in with you? She's on her own.' He was a warden.

'What's it like?' we asked.

'It's pretty bad. I don't know what's happening anywhere.'

We had her in. She wouldn't come under the table. She sat up in the chair. My father was down in Somerset. One of his parents was not well. He rang up a shop in Wareham to see if we were alright, as he thought Wareham had been flattened. We were all a bit frightened!"

Ethel Kitcat's family also sought refuge under the kitchen table, though her father had built them a shelter in the garden. The table was big and back against the wall, so they put a mattress down under it and Ethel and her children used to sleep there. On one occasion during a bad raid she was persuaded by her father-in-law to go down to the garden shelter, so "I picked up my baby Joan and carried her down. We had a cot mattress in the back of the shelter, and I put her there. When the bomb went down in Jones's Pit, the blast blew all the dirt from it through the shelter doorway and covered us." That did it, and Ethel took her baby back indoors!

It was under the stairs for the Axons, who lived in Nundico. "Mum used to put a mattress under the stairs, and me, my sister and brother used to go there when the siren went." For Doris Fooks's mum at the *Antelope,* who was always terrified when the siren went, it was under the table.

Over at Ridge, Oily Green and his family had to run down the garden whenever the siren went and hide under the bank there and, a mile or so away, the Smiths of Slepe Farm sheltered behind the ancient wall of their living room.

Within the town the Council provided public shelters, especially after Sir John Anderson announced in 1940 that the government were giving away no more Anderson shelters. Built of brick and concrete, they were to be for up to fifty residents of a single street, or at least that was the idea for the big cities. Not all Wareham's public shelters were like this. John Symonds recalled that one was below a private house on St. John's Hill, next to the *Horse and Groom*. "It was open to anyone."

Ethel Kitcat spoke of the time when the siren went when she was shopping. "A policeman came across. 'Siren's gone, my dears,' he said. 'I think you'd better go down under,' pointing to the public shelter in the *Red Lion* cellars. We took the pram down and when we got it down there was water up round our ankles. The cellars were flooded!"

When war was first declared, "everyone dived for cover." Ethel said it reminded her sister "of a whole lot of rabbits running for shelter!"

Ray Herridge explained, "Some prat rang the church bells (the pre-arranged signal that the Germans had landed.) I was a King's Messenger, along with others, and we were all looking up as if expecting to see Germans coming. They never did … We used to hide under the North Bridge during air-raids – at first. Later on, you never took any notice… You could go down on South Bridge when the Gerries used to come over and watch the sky," or up onto the North Walls near the Bowling Green to see the flashing of the AA gun at Tantinoby. "You weren't alone. There were loads of people from Edward's Crescent, up there watching!"

Harold also recalled going up on the Walls, this time at the top of Roper's Lane, where he lived see the incendiaries dropping all over the Common and bursting into flames. Ron Axon recalled how his family would go outside their house and see the flashes of the AA gun and the glare of the searchlight at Northmoor. When the gun fired, "our house used to shake!" and this would have been true for many other houses in the town.

"One night", said Ron, "father was outside watching all the 'sparklers', and a bomb came down with a high-pitched screeching whistle. He dived indoors and hid his head under the table! It was an incendiary which used to be dropped in a big canister. This opened and let out its little bombs, and this, the canister, is what father heard, nothing explosive!"

During the day there were plenty of dog-fights to watch. Harold recalled how his parents and sister used to come to meet him after Sunday School on a Sunday afternoon and they all used to walk down the river path to Ridge and have tea at Ridge, from where they could see the dog-fights.

Another basic need for the authorities was to organise the local defence should the country be invaded as, indeed, the government fully believed. As early as 1935, the Home Office, mindful of the devastation wrought by Hitler's Luftwaffe in the Spanish Civil War, had outlined to local authorities measures to ensure the safety of civilians against such air attacks. Later, in 1938, with war becoming much more imminent, Chief Wardens and ARP Wardens had to be appointed. Maud Norris's husband, an old soldier from the First World War, was one of the latter. So too was Harold Rawles' dad. His patch was Roper's Lane and the top of the Walls there.

Harry Spencer, of Bowles and Spencer, the bakers in Brixey's Lane, was chosen, appropriately, to be Bread Officer for the area. His job was not just to ensure that if anything happened there would be enough bread, but more importantly, that there were suitable water supplies should disaster – a direct hit, sabotage, — befall Wareham Waterworks' supply. For this reason, he came to know two or three places where the well water was good.

Harry played another important role in defence, as a Special Constable. He had been recruited just after the First World War, and had been on duty during the General Strike of 1926. Then, he had kept guard at the railway station to ensure no body tried to run off with the rails! But there had been no trouble and both sides had remained friendly. As a Special during the war, Harry's main job was, perhaps, the butt of many a music hall comedian. He had to see that blackout regulations were being observed, and there were no lights visible after dark.

But it was the Home Guard that is, in many people's minds, still remembered as the vital organisation of defence. On the Sunday or the Monday after war was declared, word went out for anyone who could use a rifle to join the Home Guard. They had to register at their local police station. With his experience of using Enfield rifles in the First World War, Percy Best was one of those who went to register. So too, was Charlie Damer, who had been taught to use a Lewis Machine Gun during his six months in the Territorials. Along with thousands of other men all over the country, they were all now part of the Land Defence Volunteers, the LDVs, or the "Look, Duck, and Vanish!" as they soon became popularly known.

Men everywhere were encouraged to join their local platoon. Sandford Pottery had its own, which Captain Shaw ensured all his workers there joined. Wareham

Railway had enough men for a separate platoon. Ethel Kitcat's husband and Edie Joyce's dad were also in the Home Guard. So too, was Ted Brewer.

Thus the Home Guard came into being. Their activities were later immortalised in the BBC TV series *Dad's Army*. For Ray Herridge, the real life Home Guard was just like that portrayed in the David Croft/ Jimmy Perry series, but for Percy Best and Herbie Elmes the real thing was a good deal funnier! All three Wareham men thoroughly enjoyed their time with the volunteers, describing their colleagues as "absolutely marvellous!" (Ray)

Recognised at first by only their armbands and armed with pitchforks, or whatever they could find at home, the new recruits were put through weekly sessions of drilling, either in the Drill Hall or on Wareham Common. On the latter, they were often accompanied by gangs of children who came to see what was going on. Among them was Ray Herridge. "We, as children, were absolute nuisances (as) we followed them about." David Grant was also amused by them. He was then a teenager about to leave school, and what struck him was not LDVs' show of physical prowess, but their comic appearance. "They never seemed to get their spats right or their hats!" he commented.

After one of these evening sessions, Ted Brewer came back to his pub annoyed and disgruntled. His group had been down to the riverbank, where they had had to shift logs from one place to another. This had upset Ted. He was even more mortified when the officer in charge had shouted "Brewer, get on with it!" Ted complained to his family later that he had never been spoken to like that before!

Later on, in addition to these weekly sessions, regular weekend training was held at, for example, Norton, where the army already had a camp. Hidden in the trees here was a big Howitzer gun on a railway track. Ken Ford recalled many training days, often with Bert Brown in charge. Bert Axon, Ron's father, was also an early volunteer, so too was Harold Rawles' dad. He often used to spend some time on rifle practice at the Holme Range. His son went along as well and did so well that he was picked for the Dorset Higher Grade Challenge Cup, which he won. He won the following year as well. This stood him in good stead when he later joined the RAF, and found himself picked for the regiment rifle team.

Ray Watkins was another who became very proficient with a rifle. His father was in Captain Shaw's company at Sandford, and he used to bring home a little rifle, a Mossburg, a little 2.2 gun, "a beautiful little gun. Dad and I went out of a Sunday morning to the Pottery. On the other side of the Morden road, there was a huge hole where they'd taken all the clay out, and we'd fire at targets –put up a target and fire. We'd got in all the practice we could."

Right at the beginning of the war Percy Best joined. He was one of the first to

volunteer, at a time before most men saw the urgency. Shortly after he had done so, he had a visit from Sammy Bye, the local butcher, who had taken command of one of the units.

"You're on duty, tonight, Perce, "he stated.

"Oh, duty? Where?"

"This Home Guard that you've put your name down for."

Bet, Percy and Brian Best, 1940. Percy had been in the Home Guard a few months but Brian had been connected with the Fire Service for a long time as a messenger boy. [Author's collection]

"Yes."

"Well. We've got a rota made out. You and Chuff Willey and myself, we're doing an all night duty up at the waterworks."

"Oh, are we?"

"Yes!"

"What about rifles and ammunition? No good guarding the waterworks with walking sticks."

"Oh," answered Sammy," we've got some rifles. We're to call at the Electric House (29 West Street). The big white chief there is going to issue rifles and ammunition."

The 'big white chief' was Major Archibald Carick, whose address, as area manager to the Poole Electric Co. Ltd., is given in *Kelly's Directory For Dorsetshire, 1939,* as Electric House, although some informants are certain he lived on West Walls. At the outbreak of war he was appointed Quartermaster for Wareham.

That evening Percy prepared for his long first night's duty. "I put on my overcoat, put some sandwiches in my pocket and off I went … met Sammy up at the Electric House and got a rifle and some ammunition … no slings or anything … and covered with grease." Thus armed, the two set off up the road to Worgret and the object of the patrol.

"Where's Chuff Willey, then?" asked Percy.

"Oh, they've got to work on a bit at the Bank. He won't be up here till eleven o'clock."

"Told Hitler all this then? Does he know?" asked Percy in amused sarcasm.

When they reached the waterworks they went in and found the old sergeant who was the engineer there and got half a gallon of paraffin to clean the rifle and the ammunition with. Once they had got the gun respectable, there was the problem of how to carry it. It had no sling. Percy managed to find a bit of rope and fashioned a sling from that. Then they divided out the area between them. "Sammy took to walking around the reservoir, and I took the road."

By this time, Chuff had arrived. "We had been walking around for a bit and nothing had happened. The rope (of the sling) was beginning to cut into my shoulder, so I said to Chuff,

"You want to have this rifle and carry it for a bit? It's cutting my shoulder. We've no proper slings."

So he took it.

"Never done anything like this before. What happens if we see some suspicious characters?" Chuff asked.

"Oh!" I said, "The standard thing is to shout 'Halt! Stop! Who goes there? Stand and be recognised!' If he doesn't stop, just shoot him!"

"What's he given us?"

"Five rounds of ammunition."

"I've never handled this before," Chuff said, "You'd better have it back again!" And he would not carry the damned thing any more, so I got lumbered with it!

I said, "I've got some sandwiches."

He said, "Drink in the car."

"OK!" so I got into the car and had my sandwiches and a bottle of beer. After a time, I said "OK! Sam, it's quiet now. You and Chuff can have a lie down."

They went to the car, and Sammy came running back.

"Here," he said, "what have you done with that bottle of beer?"

"I found a bottle so I drank it."

"That was between the three of us!"

So the night dragged on, until by about half past four or five the sky was beginning to grow lighter and people were starting to move around.

"We could stand down now." Sammy called.

"Don't see what we've been doing up here all night," commented Percy.

All three of them piled into Chuff's car and started off down the hill back to the town. As they drew near to the new Senior School, they found a road block erected across their way, guarded by soldiers of the King's Own. One of them called the driver to halt.

"Can you identify yourselves?"

"We couldn't!" recalled Percy years later, "But we told them who we were and what we had been doing. The chap was very suspicious, especially when he found five rounds of ammunition and an old rifle in the car!"

"'Afraid you can't go by. We shall have to find someone who can say who you are."

He called to one of the guards, who accompanied Sammy, Percy and Chuff down the road and into South Street Police Station, where the three were quickly identified and allowed to go home.

On the fourth night of his duty, some real old characters of the town joined Percy. They were Bert Whittle, Skinny Whittle, and Walter Rose. All three were prominent butchers of the town and came along armed with a double-barrelled shotgun each.

"What's the big idea?," enquired Percy.

"Well, we thought that there are a lot of rabbits up there in the morning. If you'd like to stay on guard duty here, the two of us'll slip up the road, one of us driving, and the other could have a couple of rabbits with it!

And that's what we did. I stayed. Skinny and Walter went up the road and came back with about three rabbits."

Walter was a real character. On another occasion, fairly early in the war, Percy and Walter were returning from another night duty and coming down the Worgret Road one morning, when they heard noises coming from the other side of the road.

"We'll nip across and see who it is!" There was a lot of coughing and spluttering going on.

"Come out of there!" yelled Walter, brandishing his gun. "Whoever you are, with your hands up! If you don't come out, I'm going to shoot!"

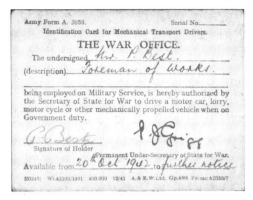

Percy Best's permit allowing him to drive a W.D. car whilst on duty. 20th October 1942 [Author's collection]

By and by a figure emerged from the bushes.

"You be too keen to use that rifle!" I said. "Let's see who it is we've got first!"

It turned out to be a sergeant on a searchlight unit who had been into Wareham for a bite and had had a skinful, and went to relieve himself behind the bushes and had slipped and fallen and couldn't get out"

On other occasions, to relieve the monotony of a long uneventful night's duty, Walter would bring up an air-rifle, and they would all take pot-shots at some beehives that old Bill Sergeant, the waterwork's manager, kept up there. "You had to do something to pass the time away!" commented Percy. Fortunately, for him and his companions, "the weather was nice and kind"

Once when they were on duty, they spotted a light – crime of all crimes at that time – at Wareham Station. So Walter rang up.

"Quartermaster Mr. Carick!"

"Yes?" came the answer.

"There's a light on Wareham Station and it should not be showing!
Put it out, will you, please!"

Five minutes passed, or perhaps it was ten, and the light still shone brightly. Walter rang again.

"Carick!" he bellowed, "That bloody light's still on down there!
If it's not out in five minutes, I'm going to shoot!"

They waited. Five minutes dragged by, but the light still showed no signs of going out. Walter, in exasperation, picked up his gun and let rip. "The bullets couldn't, of course, have reached the mile down to the station, but the light went out!" Percy recalled.

When Brian Best was about ten, he badly wanted to go with his father on night duty. Percy tried for a long time to put him off by saying it was a long night. Brian persisted, so Percy relented and took him. He sat him on a stool that Percy had taken so he could watch the searchlights, until about midnight when he could keep awake no longer, and fell asleep in his dad's arms. Walter said, "Bring him down, and we'll put him in the van." That's what they did, tucking him up in a blanket that was there. Years later, Brian confessed that he could still smell the stink of that butcher's van!

Across the other side of the town, Ben Watkins often did his duty on Harp Hill at Ridge, probably

Prime Minister Winston Churchill inspecting a training exercise near Wareham. [Photograph courtesy of the Imperial War Museum, London. H2278]

with Edie Joyce's dad. Here there was an observation post, an old Nissen hut for the men to shelter in. Fred Simpson seems to have been in charge. To wile away the long and tedious hours, Ben used to take along a pack of playing cards, a set of darts and some drink, all of which helped to relieve the tedium. His wife could not understand how he found this enjoyable. "I don't know what you want to go down there for!" She used to say, "There's nothing down there!" Perhaps this hut was a little more luxurious than some. It had "a tiny little stove... if they wanted to cook." (Edie)

As Charlie Damer lived out side the town he was assigned to 12 Platoon East Stoke and since he had Territorial experience, he became a Lance-Corporal. His job was, with others, to cover the Brownie Gun in the village.

Another position that was a guard point was an old shepherd's hut down at Kimmeridge.

Inside, there was an old bicycle hung up, with two flat tyres. "We had to ride that, if Jerry came, to the nearest telephone to alert the captain!" said Ken Ford.

Ken also recalled that on one occasion he was on duty with Master Michael, who was one of the Wood Family who every year leased the big house down at Arne for the summer season. On this particular night Bert Sloman, who worked on Ridge Wharf was sergeant of the guard and, noticing that Master Michael always wore a watch and chain when he arrived for duty, even when he had his overalls on, asked;-

"Wood, would you mind putting your watch on the mantelpiece, so I can see the time to change the guard?"

"It's rather an expensive watch, and I don't want to lose it," he replied, and he did not let go of it at all.

On top of St. Martin's House in North Street was another duty position. Compared with the other places, this one was well equipped; it had a machine gun.

In addition to night watches, it was also the responsibility of the Home Guard to erect anti-tank devices wherever it was thought that German tanks might be held up if the enemy did invade. The main streets of the town were obviously places for such devices, and huge holes were dug in them which were covered over. These tops had to be lifted off every time and huge iron girders – old railways lines — slipped in. According to Percy Best, it took six to eight men to lift one. "You had to manhandle them … drop them down into the hole … one leg straight down into the hole, and the other leg would be at an angle, five to six feet high. If German tanks came, they could not get over;" at least that was the theory.

To make sure they could be erected quickly and taken down again with equal speed, the Home Guard teams had to keep practising. "It became their pride and joy, to see how quickly they could get them in and out again. They got very proficient at it," commented Ray Watkins. "Dad's lot were pretty good at it." In fact the various crews used to vie with each other as to how quickly they could put up one of these defences. It was all very competitive.

The Home Guard also had to block certain areas with barbed wire. One place it was laid was across the footpath down to the river beside the Priory.

A recent Channel 4 TV documentary (December 2002) highlighted a little known aspect of war defence. Essentially it was a secret operation and information about it is only just beginning to come to light. Specially chosen people were selected and enrolled in these local units. Their essential job was to hold up Hitler's invasion of this country. Mr. Quick, who used to work at the market, was reputed to have been the leader of a small troop of volunteers who would, in the event of a German invasion and the mass exodus of all the local people, stay behind and hide in the claypits to sabotage and hold up the invasion. Could this have been part of Churchill's secret army depicted in the TV documentary?

Also part of it may have been the local farmer chosen presumably for his trustworthiness, whose farm was set up as a store for secret supplies. Tunnels were dug under the fields and stocked with ammunition and petrol in case of invasion. These passages were only known to the farmer and one or two others, which fits in well with the evidence given in the TV programme.

It was also obvious that Britain was under siege from the number of searchlights that were set up and which lit up the sky at night. Percy Best had the task of supervising their erection and their maintenance. He had been Foreman of Works and later Clerk of Works of the Royal Engineers, so he was deemed a man with experience in such things.

This meant being on call for 24 hours a day, which in turn put an end to his being in the Home Guard.

Searchlights and guns were regarded as essential in the area to protect the cordite factory at Holton Heath. It had been built during the war in 1915, but its importance in the Second World War was enormous. After the withdrawal of British troops from Dunkirk it became one of the major targets for German planes. It produced a huge amount of cordite, essential for British defence. To put it out of action was high on German objectives, but its deliberate position, mainly underground and highly camouflaged, was not obvious from the air. But, there was still a need for guns and searchlights ringing the area.

Searchlights were set up at Lychett, Trigon, Keysworth, Arne, Kimmeridge, Winfrith and Moreton. However, this form of defence was virtually in its infancy, and so the sites were frequently re-arranged, first into single sites, and later into cluster sites of three or four lights.

For a single site, a team consisted of twelve men under a troop sergeant living on site. One hut was for sleeping; a second one acted as a dining room, and the third for recreation. All had concrete floors and were usually some distance away from the actual searchlight. Often they were hidden from view by trees and shrubs. The searchlight, of course, had to be out in the open on a site that gave the operations team as wide a scope as possible to sweep the skies with their light. The one at Arne, on the hill above the village, was typical.

Two men, the 'spotters', kept watch some distance away from the actual light and could let the light crew know by means of a field telephone when they saw an enemy plane and where it was in the sky. The light itself was powered by its own generator, which, like the huts, was placed out of sight and some distance away.

For practically the whole of the war these sites were operated by the 5th Battery of the 2nd Searchlight Regiment, whose headquarters was at St. Martin's House, the old Filliter home in North Street. This was requisitioned at the beginning of the war, but the soldiers who manned the lights were billeted in various houses around the town.

To support the searchlights Light Ack-Ack and Heavy Ack-Ack units were set up where it was thought they were most needed, and one obvious place was the cordite factory at Holton Heath. Road blocks were erected at Kingsbridge at the east end of the site and at Digby's Corner, where the Organford road turned off the main road.

The headquarters of the Battery occupying the factory defences was in Sandford House, the old Fillieul home, now requisitioned.

There were eight sites for the L.A.A. units, at West Heath, Sandford House, Lone Pine, Kingsbridge and Fox Hill, all just inside the factory perimeter, and at the jetty, East Holton Farm and Arne, outside. At Sandford House and at West Heath, two concrete towers were built to counteract any low flying aircraft. They were some thirty feet high. One tower had the gun, a power operated Bofor, and the other acted as an ammunition store.

As daylight raids on the area increased, mobile units were introduced to move around the area, but these did not require Percy Best's R.E. assistance.

The Heavy Ack-Ack units came under a different control. Their headquarters and control room was at Lychett Manor, former home of the Lee Family, now requisitioned. Earlier, some damage had been done to their house during a raid, when the farmer, Alec Lockyer, had lost several cows.

A H.A.A. gun near Wareham. [Photograph courtesy of the Imperial War Museum, London. H7567]

There were four more or less permanent sites of these Heavy Ack-Ack units, all coded "Harry", and numbered 1, 2, 3 and 4. Harry 1, situated on Arne peninsula, was a four gun site. Later it was converted into a six gun remote controlled site. Here, between 130 to 150 men could be housed in its wooden huts that were screened from view by trees. Situated as it was on a hill, the main difficulty here, and at Harry 3 as well, was the lack of a water supply, but at Arne a good supply was found at Gold Point, which necessitated pumps and an engine being installed to supply water to 5,000 gallon Braithwaite tanks. Sewage proved at little more difficult to solve, but fortunately the soil was very sandy and absorbent. So, with careful laying of pipes the sewage was taken onto the heath, and this seemed to work satisfactorily. Life at Harry 1 has been dealt with in *Arne, A Purbeck Parish in Peace and War.*

Harry 2 was at Northport, between what was Tantinoby Lane and the Golf Course, and, as at Arne, was originally a four

Churchill inspects. [Photograph courtesy of the Imperial war Museum, London. H2277]

gun site. Later, again , as at Arne, it had two more guns added. Living accommodation was similar to that at Arne, but being near the town, water supply was not a problem. The site was connected to the town's water pipes and to its sewers. At that time the pressure of the town's supply was low during the daytime, and again Braithwaite tanks were used.

As the war progressed and manpower became a problem, mixed batteries came to Harry 2, 3 and 4. The arrival of A.T.S. had, of course, considerable effect on the accommodation, and alterations had to be made in sleeping, bathing, and toilets. Lady Digby was asked to supervise these adaptations. For a while the N.A.A.F.I. had a base there at Harry 2.

Harry 3 and 4 were much the same as Harry 2. Harry 3 was situated at Slepe Farm near Organford, on the left hand side of the Poole/Dorchester Road. Harry 4 was located on what was heathland on the east side of the Poole/Blandford Road at Upton. This was an easier site to manage in that, like the Northport site, it had plenty of water, but a drainage system had to be built, especially when the A.T.S. moved in.

For a time, a superior Heavy Artillery unit was stationed in the town, in huts built in St Martin's Lane and close to the Church School there. It had its headquarters on the Grange Road, in Pike's bungalow there. For this unit, a siding was constructed at Norden off the railway to Swanage and a big gun – "a really big gun," according to Percy Best –was installed on the top of Creech Barrow. Its unit had their accommodation at Norden, but as the war progressed and the threat of invasion passed, the camp here found a use as a home for Italian prisoners.

As Percy Best was in fairly close contact with all these units, it did mean that he met some interesting people. For a time, there was a Sportmen's Battery, in which some top class sportsmen were to be met, cricketers, footballers and jockeys (the Wragg Brothers). Its PT instructor was Jack Patterson, a former British heavy weight champion. Percy was very embarrassed on one occasion. He was well known in the area as a referee for local soccer matches for local lads and for the fire brigade. He was therefore in great demand, although he had no qualifications. No one seemed to mind. On one occasion he handed over one of the gun sites to a Major Nichols who asked Percy if he would referee on the following Sunday a match against a sister battery.

"Yes," said Percy reluctantly, "if you'll provide the transport."

"OK," agreed the Major.

"So on Sunday, I was collected by the Sergeant Major and transported over to Sandford House. He left me to go and change into football togs. We met up again and had to pass through the farm to the soccer pitch — now, the Sandford School playing field – when I saw a number of officers including a colonel walking around the teams kicking a ball around.

I said to the Sergeant Major, "Not the first time these lads have kicked a ball around!'

'No,' he said, 'they are all professionals.'

'Are you a pro?'

'Yes. I play centre forward for Aberdeen.'

I wondered what he'd let me in for, but I need not have had any worries. It was easier than controlling a lads' game!"

The presence of the army was very much in evidence all around the town, as Edie Joyce explained, "If you went out, when you came back, they'd stop you.

'Halt! Who goes there?'

And you had to say 'A friend!' and they'd let you through."

But the army's presence was not new. During the First World War, there had been a large army camp on the Worgret Road. The demands of the soldiers there for food, recreation, and laundry services, among other things, had boosted local trade, so that when the authorities decided to move the camp to Bovington sometime after the war, it was a serious blow to the town's economy.

The coming of war in 1939 was once again to fill the town with soldiers. Cornishman F. George came with a whole host of others to Wareham. Many of his fellows moved onto a new camp at Arne: F. George and others were based at another new camp near the station at Tantinoby.

He remembered Wareham as a "great town", with "nice people. We used to sing in a pub." Fellow Cornishman, Don Gilbert, who was stationed at Arne, often used to get into town with his mates. He was lucky. His friend, Len Oliver, owned a small Austin 10, and at weekends as many as it could hold would pile into the car and go into Wareham. Other soldiers from Arne had to walk the four miles in and the four miles out. For Don, it was the *Black Bear* that was his favourite pub. Often, they had time to slip into the little teashop near the bridge, Burgess's, "run by two very nice ladies"

At their house at the entrance to Holton Heath the Thompsons "always had troops." Bob Thompson recalled that his sister, June, was always bringing in her soldier friends and her friend Joyce, who lived in the flats up the road, was always dropping in with a soldier. Bob said, "If I walked in and found a soldier there, I didn't bother."

"We had one chap brought in, he'd cut his leg pretty badly, and Mum said;- 'Bring him in here!' So we got him picked up and brought in, until an ambulance could fetch him."

With a large army presence in the area, it was not surprising that many houses were requisitioned. St. Martin's and Sandford Houses and Lytchett Manor have already been mentioned. Several others were taken over as well. The garage on the North Causeway became the repair centre for army wagons and lorries as well as being a petrol filling station for the military. The old lodging house at the foot of St. Martin's Hill became a store, and, in North Street, 'Peter Pan' Cottage, the Manse, the Methodist Schoolroom, and part of the *Red Lion* were also taken over. Across the road, Godwin's fruitshop was used as a billet for the Forestry Section of the Women's Land Army, while in South Street, Bridge House became a food and recreation centre, run by the WVS. Opposite to it, Holy Trinity was requisitioned for a time, and a scheme drawn up to turn it into a NAFFI, but that was later dropped and the building remained empty.

In East Street, the house on the corner of Bonnet's Lane was also taken over, and for a time, the military police even had a bedroom in the *King's Arms*.

The army's presence was felt in other ways about the town. Gun places were made in East and West Streets and at Mrs Coffin's house at the bottom of Bell's Orchard, the ceiling was shored up and its windows made removable, so that the army could install a machine gun upstairs there. Tanks were always roaming through the main streets, so much so that road surfaces could not cope and had to be strengthened. Occasionally a tank broke down. Audrey Richards spoke about a Churchill tank that came off its tracks and became stuck in a field near where she lived. Her parents had to put the crew up in their tiny cottage for several days.

"You know what rations were like!" she recently recalled. "We were right down to the bread line. Our neighbours helped us out. (Eventually) they sent a GS wagon loaded up with food for us. They couldn't repair the tank so they left it!"

Pill Boxes were constructed at the four main entrances to the old town. That guarding St

One of the houses requisitioned, seen being repainted in 2002. [Author's collection]

Martin's Pitch is still there, between the Church and what was the *Lord Nelson*, while the one for the south end of the town, guarding the Causeway and the bridge, was on Abbot's Quay.

At one time, Wareham was going to have a large petrol, oil and lubricant depot, and a considerable amount of research was carried out on a possible site at West Holme, but the idea was dropped when the gunnery wing of the R.T.C. wanted to extend their ranges in the Holme area and the depot was established at West Moors. Later, there was another possibility of building the depot at Trigon, but that too was dropped.

Early in the war, the Headmaster of the Upper School, Mr Bricknell decided with another member of staff, Mr. Stuckey, to form a group of army cadets. Ray Watkins and David Grant were among the early volunteers. "We had a smashing time really," recalled David recently, "We used to go to Dorchester Barracks now and then for weekends. We went to camps at Dewlish and Iwerne Minster, near Blandford." Harold Rawles added that Bovington Camp was another venue, where "we had a go on the tanks!" This was a tremendous thrill for the lads. In Wareham, Ray Herridge said they used "to fire at a tank gun with a big red rubber thing. We used to fire over the bridge, and I remember once we hit the bridge, one of the alcoves, and the thing ricocheted off." Ray Watkins got on well and was promoted to a sergeant major, a great honour of which he was proud.

Harold also told of going with Mr. Stuckey on several occasions to Somerfield Airfield over at Christchurch where they could go flying and learn how to pilot a craft. Perhaps it was this experience that made him elect to join the RAF when his time came. He was doing so well he was all set to take his pilot's licence when he was called up.

The older cadets were allowed to go with the Home Guard when they went up on the ranges in Holme Lane, which were relics of the First World War. Here Ray and David learnt how to fire a 303 rifle and a Sten Gun, as well as the more usual 202 rifles that were usually used in practice.

Another venture started at the school was the Air Training Corps. Ron Axon complained that they did not do much. He was very disappointed that they could not go flying. Aircraft observation was what they had to practise and they had charts up on the walls showing various planes. Occasionally, there were other things, which Ron found far more exciting. "Once we were taken to Wool on the back of a six-wheeled lorry with the baseball team to watch them play the soldiers." The trip seemed to be a great adventure for the lads. "Once a year we used to go to Swanage on the train with the Sunday School trip. Any other time we never used to go anywhere, but to get in the back of that lorry and go five or six miles out of Wareham was great!" However, Ron "did not go on with it after I left school," he said, "but others did" and were taken over to RAF Locking (the RAF Helicopter Centre today) near Weston-super-Mare. Here they went up in planes such as the de Havilland Rapid, which was a great experience.

Mr. Bricknell was the instigator of Wareham's branch of the ATC. Harold Rawles was one of its enthusiastic young volunteers. At first he was slightly too young to be a member, but Mr. Bricknell allowed him to go along. When he was old enough, he was allowed his uniform, and very proud of it he was. After Mr Bricknell's death, "an army bloke, Major Carick took over." His activities with the Home Guard have already been mentioned.

Wareham Army Cadets, 1944-5 David Grant is sitting on the extreme left. Ray Watkins, Sergeant Major, had been called up for the mines when this was taken. [David Grant]

A year or so before the war began, his son, Alan, used to entertain Wareham people on Sunday afternoons when he gave aerial displays over the town in his yellow plane. Unfortunately, during the war he failed to return from a bombing mission.

His father, the Major,

was a military man and tried to instill more discipline in the teenagers, but, Harold remembered, he did used to take them to Bovington. Others who were concerned in running the ATC were Mr. Garland and Seymour Lee.

Proud father and his children: Albert Axon of the Home Guard in Wareham; Ron in the uniform of the ATC 2051 Squadron and June in her Civil Defence uniform. She used to do night duty at Westport House. [Ron Axon]

When it was first mooted about using army cadets to help the Home Guard, it was thought they could be very useful to have messenger-boys attached to the pill boxes. Ray was attached to his father's box in East Street. The first time he was allowed to take part was the practice night, when the regular army planned a surprise attack on Wareham; a surprise in that "we didn't know from which direction. As it happened, they came from the east, from Poole Harbour.

'Here's a message. Take it up to Glebe House,' he was told. 'Glebe House in North Street was where the headquarters had been set up. I raced up to North Street, got to Glebe House, and was just about to go in when a bloke grabbed me by the scruff.

'Where are you going?'

'I've got to go in there with a message!'

'You can't go in there!'

'I'm a messenger boy!'

'I don't care who you are!' and he wouldn't let me in! I had to go all the way back.

'Did you tell 'em?' they asked.

'No. They wouldn't let me in!'

'What do you mean? They wouldn't let you in?'

Ray then explained what had happened.

'Stupid man! We'll have to do something about him!'

Next I knew some officials from Headquarters came down to see how the practice was progressing, and they were told that we missed everything since I was not let in. There was a postmortem, and it was agreed that we messenger boys should have some means of identification."

Just as the Home Guard may seem to us today to have lived up to its TV reputation, so Wareham Fire Brigade seemed before the war to have been a relic of some past century. Indeed, if the Yanks had arrived in the town in the twenties, they would have found it very antiquated and comical, with its horse-drawn water wagon and hand pump. They might well have imagined they had arrived on the film set for the Keystone Cops. The fire engine was kept in what is now the Granary Restaurant, and the horse pastured across the river. In the town's defence, and to be fair to the earnest men who formed the brigade, it should be pointed out that Wareham was no worse in this respect than many other towns up and down the country.

The crew of ten men and their captain were all amateur part-time firemen, who had other jobs to do. Joe Barnes was a plumber and the Symonds brothers chimney sweeps. All were there to fight fires certainly, but also to enjoy themselves, and sometimes that got the better of them.

When there was a fire, the bell on top the almshouses in East Street was pulled and the alarm sounded. If it occurred at night, then the men would have to be woken up. Jack Spiller was a teenager when he joined the crew and he was often given the job of cycling round. The Symonds brothers lived in Church Street in a thatched cottage the front entrance of which was down three steps. By standing on the pedals of his bike Jack could tap the windows to wake them.

The brigade, with Harry Newbery the blacksmith as its Captain had to go and find George Cox who was often pulling wood around the town as they wanted his horse for the fire engine. While he went to fetch the horse from the other side of the river where it was roaming, the others pulled the engine out onto the Quay, with its collapsible buckets, which had leather handles. It was always filled with water from the hand pump on Abbot's Quay.

In essence, it was a machine that had not changed since the eighteenth century, or even before. They had a choice of two machines, the smaller four handle manual pump, which is now in the Dorset County Museum, or the larger eight handle manual pump. When the horse arrived, it had to be fixed in the shafts and then they could set off for the fire. Fortunately, the town never had a serious fire, so in a sense the system lasted.

At some time between the wars, Harry Newbery had made some new shafts, but when the horse was put between them it was too big. Faced with this dilemma, Cox went back to his timber wagon, sending two or three men on over to Stoborough and the fire on their bicycles. Taking the shafts off his wagon, Cox carried them back to the Quay, where he fastened them onto the fire wagon and the engine set off. The remaining couple of firemen climbed on board, much to the delight of a group of children who had congregated around as soon as they had heard the fire bell. Among them was the young Herbie. He and his friends liked to jump on the back of the engine. This they now did. All was well until the

The old fire engine being borrowed in 1933 by the Muddlecombe Men. The town council then discovered the town was not insured if the engine was out of town taking part in carnival processions. That led to Wareham having a modern fire engine [Herbie Elmes collection]

engine came to the humped back bridge that led over the river (until 1927). Here the animal had no strength to pull engine, men and the lads on the back and the horse came to a stop.

"Everybody get off!" yelled Cox.

All did so, and rushed to the back of the engine and began to push. Gradually the horse and engine moved up and over the hump. Then everybody climbed back on.

"Get off," yelled Cox, "Only the firemen!" and so all the kids jumped off.

"Some time later," Herbie related, "a car came across from Stoborough and stopped the policeman by the bridge.

'What's up?' he asked.

'The hoses have leaked! They want to borrow some from the station."

The motorist said he was going over to the station and would bring their hoses back.

"Presently we see the motorist come back again. The policeman asked him again. A crowd was there waiting to see what was happening

'Station hoses don't fit their pumps!"

The fire was put out. Fortunately, it did not do much damage except to the farmer's hayrick! It did not involve lives.

Once between the wars after Swanage had modernised its service with an up-to-date machine, officials there had contacted Wareham to know if the town wanted to pay a retaining fee and then they could have the use of the new Swanage fire-engine. Wareham had turned down the offer, arguing that they had never really had a large fire, and the existing service was adequate to deal with the little fires they suffered. As a result, the new engine never came Wareham side of Corfe.

Another story Herbie Elmes used to tell was of the occasion when smoke was seen coming billowing across the gravestones from the boiler room of Lady St. Mary's, and the fire brigade was summoned. It was decided that water would have to be got from the garden of Davis Row, opposite, and a chain gang was set up. Herbie recalled two of the team were Mr Lacey with his wooden leg and farmer Lucas, neatly attired with bowler hat and umbrella. Herbie watched as Lucas with his umbrella on his arm carried an empty bucket, which he handed on and then took a full one back to Lacey, who hopped along with it. While this was going on, Harry Newbery, the brigade captain, arrived with Frank Arnold, one of his assistants.

Frank shouted, "Let me go, Captain! Let me go in!"

"No," the captain replied, "I can't risk a life like that."

But Frank kept on, "Let me go in.!"

"No," the captain said, "We'll get some water. We'll get a drop of water first."

Still the smoke was billowing out.

Frank said, "Put a rope round me," and the captain agreed with this, and in Frank went, only to be yanked out again as quickly as he went in!

"What are you doing?" he yelled. "I haven't had a look round yet."

"I thought you was overcome," came the reply.

"I'm alright, Captain. I'll shout when I want to come out," and in he went again.

The captain waited a few minutes and then said, "He's very quiet in there. Bring a bucket of water up the front and chuck a bucket in!" Another yank on the rope and out came Frank once more.

"I haven't had a chance, Captain. Let me go in!"

This went on for sometime, before the Swanage Fire Brigade was called, and the fire was put out. It cost Wareham £25 for the help. It seemed that the fire had started in a heap of coal ready for the boiler. A cigarette may have been responsible.

Another incident that Herbie told related to time when the brigade could not find a source of water. A fire started at the rear of Symonds' shop at 7 West Street. Fred Symonds had taken over the flourishing printer's and stationer's shop after James Tribblett had died in 1917, an establishment that went back in these premises certainly to 1823, when Peter Groves is mentioned in an early directory. Nearby, Mr Chaffey, who had a sweetshop, was out the back attempting to save his galvinised garage with a half inch hose pipe, hoping to get some water, but pressure that day was low. In the street a crowd had gathered, but Herbie said few were bothering to help get water. Every so-often, firemen with handkerchiefs tied over their face came galloping up, in despair about not being able to find water. Then, some disappeared next door into George Paul's high quality drapery and tailor's shop (9 - 11 West Street). This was another well established business. Paul had been there since before 1885, and had taken over from John Tasker, who set up there before 1830.

"The firemen," said Herbie, "were gone some time in Paul's, and then another lot came galloping out, shouting 'Where's the hydrants?'"

Meanwhile Johnny Trimarco and his crowd were searching one street and Gus Symonds went up West Street. This went on for some time. Eventually, they put the fire out. It had been started by a cigarette, or by a spark from a steamroller."

A report in the *Dorset County Chronicle* for 8th January 1931 suggests that Herbie's stories are not that exaggerated. It is a highly scathing attack on the town's service, describing the place where the engine was kept as "a wood shed….rather like an artist's studio, or converted barn." Of the engine itself, "it would be better in a museum than elsewhere. It could probably not cast a jet of water over the town's highest building. … When fire breaks out in this delightful spot, they ring a bell. It hangs on a wooden frame on the almshouse roof. This is a quaint, moss-covered building. …If a fire is obliging enough to start before the ancients have gone to bed, things move comparatively swiftly. When it occurs after sundown, the inmates must be awakened before the bell can be rung, since, on retiring, they lock their front door. And this door gives access to the bell-ladder. On hearing the summons, the brigade makes from all points

Herbie Elmes in September 1992 - the year of his death. [Hughie Elmes]

for the fire station. Some of them live at considerable distances away, and invariably time is lost on the journey. Then the horses have to be brought to the engine and harnessed. And then Wareham's fire brigade sets forth to fight the flames. At one fire, a member appeared without his helmet. When asked the reason by the Captain he explained that going to the peg in the fire-shed, where his helmet was hung, he found a hen nesting in his headgear. 'Of course, cap'n, I couldn't disturb she.' Actually when a serious outbreak occurs, they send for the Poole motor pump."

This system continued for a sometime after this, but, when Herbie joined the fire service just before the war, it had improved out of all recognition. Gone was the horse drawn vehicle, and in its place was a new modern motorised fire engine. The service now had a proper station of its own, specially built for it on St John's Hill on the site of the seventeenth century chapel, where the new engine was kept.

The reason which Jack Spiller suggested for the change was that on the last time the firemen went to get the horse from its field, it had become stuck fast in one of the ponds over there and had to be pulled out, which lost valuable time. As a result of this incident, Jack reckoned the Council decided it was time to order a new engine.

Thus, it was a very important day for the town when Jack accompanied the Mayor and Harry Kirk, the Town Clerk, up to Luton where the new engine was built, to take possession of it. They were given "a wonderful reception at Luton," said Jack.

The men were now expected to go down the station each week, for which they received three shillings (15p.) in payment. Tuesday nights was drill night as well as Sunday mornings. Herbie had a lot of respect for Captain Newbery. He was an expert at putting out heath fires, which were a frequent occurrence around Wareham, but some of his men often pulled his leg unmercifully.

On one occasion, at the beginning of the war, he had had an official letter about the possible use by the Germans of mustard gas, the dreadful poison gas that was used to devastating effect in the First World War, and the Government were frightened something like this would be used again.

Captain Newbery called his men together and explained, "Eventually, when it (the gas) comes down, it hits the ground and spreads out ever so carefully. It don't come very high."

Frankie Arnold, who worked as a blacksmith for him, and always game for a laugh, said, "You mean, something like cow shit then, Captain?"

"Well...yes ... something like that, Frank"

"Well, couldn't we cut some inner tubes up and put them in rings, like elastic bands, and pull them over our boots and round our legs to stop it creeping up our legs?"

"Good idea, Frank," agreed the Captain. Herbie did not record whether they did take up Frank's suggestion seriously.

Another of Herbie's stories concerned a call out the brigade had on a Sunday. "Two or three gangs had gone out. We're down there and we're sitting about. Suddenly a car pulled up and a girl driving. In comes the Chief Officer!

'What are you doing?' he asked.

'We're next in line to go out.'

'Well,' he yelled, 'get your pumps ready, and stand to attention when you speak to me! Right! Get the pump out and get it ready for the next go-out!'

Then, the bell went

'Right! Off you go!'

So we went! One chap, Len Christopher said, ' I never drove this thing before. I suppose it'll be alright?'

We got halfway to Stoborough, and the driver said, 'Where's us going?'

'Damn me, I never asked!…. Drive on till you see some smoke!' we drove all round the Purbecks till 9 o'clock that night. Never see anything of smoke, or fire, or anything else. We came back. No one said anything!"

The withdrawal of British troops from France at Dunkirk meant that Hitler's armies were just across the Channel and could invade at any moment. Urgent changes had to be made, and the brigade became part of the National Fire Service. That meant other changes; another fire officer came from Weymouth to take over the Wareham Brigade, which now became responsible for a much wider area, the whole of the South West Purbecks, Corfe, Bere Regis in the west and curving round Poole over to Ferndown in the east, a large important section of Dorset. "We slept down (at the station) many nights," recalled Herbie. A concrete room was specially built with bunks in when the Germans began to use incendiaries."

In addition, the station now became the headquarters for the fire service from Sixpenny Handley in the north to Swanage in the south. Even Brownsea Island came under its auspices. A control centre was built in its loft, which was managed during the war period by Emily Newbery and her staff of four girls. Each was on duty for a period of 48 hours and then had 24 hours off.

The apparatus in the area was under her control, so she was able to call out whatever was required. Each appliance was given a tally, so she could see at a glance which appliances were already in use and where the spares ones were. Many retired firemen have paid tribute to her efficiency.

In addition to the engine, the station had a mobile dam capable of holding 36 gallons of water and a trailer pump to get the water out. One problem the area did face was the lack of hydrants. Usually if the fire was in the town, the waterworks were informed, so that they could boost the supply to the hydrants.

In the event of a fire outside, the nearest water supply had to be located. Another difficulty was that Wareham did not have an engine with an escape ladder, but if one was needed, Poole could be asked to send theirs.

With the new man, Eddie Dawes, in control, "things were different." Herbie confessed.

"He sorted things out a bit, and then we were more efficient. We did practise fire drill and we got it down to seven minutes! We were absolutely proud of this. We could get on the scene, get the pump out and hose and everything, and on target in seven minutes!"

The men even wanted to enter the inter-brigade competition.

"Unfortunately, our captain said, 'I'm sorry. I don't think we've got it fine enough yet! We must carry on.'

We did carry on practising and we went to the competition, but Ringwood won! It rather let us down a bit!"

Perhaps the biggest raid the men had to deal with was the night the Germans bombed Arne, thinking they were pounding Holton Heath and its cordite factory. In the days that followed, Wareham had the job of preventing the heathland bursting into flames again and acting as a signal for the enemy planes. As Jack Spiller explained, heath fires kept breaking out over again and again. Even though they apparently seem to have been put out, such fires go underground and flare up again sometime later.

Of course, in 1939 there were other problems to deal with and the town was expected to have its share of evacuees. It was taken for granted that when war did come, Hitler would order the mass destruction of London and other British cities, just as the newsreels in the cinemas had shown he had devastated cities on the continent. Therefore, the British Government had made plans to evacuate children and expectant mothers from the areas that were likely to be Hitler's targets. When war did come, Operation Pied Piper as it was known went immediately onto action, and on September 1st, the first schoolchildren left London. It was a tremendous undertaking as during the first four days a staggering 1,334,360 children were moved out, each taking with them, as ordered, a carrier bag with three tins of meat, three of milk, a loaf of bread or a packet of biscuits and a quarter pound of chocolate.

Their foster mothers were to be paid 10s 6d (52 1/2p) for the first child and 8s 6d (42 1/2p) for each additional child (Details from Eden Camp).

The arrival at the station of those bound for Wareham was not a promising one. That Saturday, the 2nd September, as they arrived, the heavens opened and a thunderstorm threw it down! Everyone was drenched to the skin, and fed up, and longing to be home! However, the *Dorset County Chronicle* proudly announced in November 1939 that the Wareham area had received 1,642 children since the war had started.

Finding enjoyment in a glass of beer, when they could get it.....
Doris Fooks with Vernon Riggs and Eddie Anderson who both joined the navy. The lad on the right is one of the Brights, is it Johnny? Taken at the back of The Antelope.
[Doris James]

For some the drenching at the start was it, and within a few days, weeks, they had escaped back home. The *Dorset County Chronicle* reckoned some 500 had returned by the end of October. Later, in December, the paper estimated that 767 were still in the area; that was about 47% of those who originally came. This was about the national average. Figures at Eden Camp suggest that about half the number of children had left their foster districts by Christmas. Some locals complained about those who did so. According to J. Murphy in his book, *Dorset At War,* they said that those who went back left behind them a mountain of debt.

However, the Chief Billeting Officer of the area, A.T Selvey, who was Wareham's Sanitary Inspector, was more optimistic and felt that the arrangements had worked better than anyone in the town had anticipated. After all to find homes for so many children and for many expectant mothers was a tremendous task.

With so many newcomers in the area, there were bound to be difficulties. "They were a strange lot in some respects, but they didn't know where milk came from!" (Ray Herridge). Their's was a different culture. Audrey Richards remembered them asking; "Coo,! What a bloody place! Where's the pop shop?" In spite of this difference, it is perhaps surprising that many stayed on.

The blackout was one of the first things the government introduced, and all street lights in the town had to be turned off. In this, Wareham was no different to any other place at this time. It was feared that enemy planes would use street lights to guide them to strategic targets. In addition, windows of houses and shops had to have blackout material covering them when any light inside was being used.

To comply with these restrictions, shops had to close earlier. *The Dorset County Chronicle* for 21st September 1939 announced that in future all shops in the town would close on Mondays, Tuesday and Thursdays at 6 o'clock, and on Fridays at 6.30pm and Saturdays at 7.0pm. However, fruiterers, confectioners, tobacconists and stationers could stay open till 7 o'clock on weekdays and to 8.0 o'clock on Saturdays.

The Rector also brought the hour of the Sunday evening service forward to 3.15 pm to help save electricity and to save attempting to blackout the large windows of the parish church.

Rationing was another action of central government. Millions and millions of ration books were issued. Customers had to sign up with a specific grocer to obtain their basic supplies, and they could not go anywhere else for these things. Shops ran campaigns urging their customers to act quickly and register. During the first year of the war, rationing was restricted to sugar, butter, fats, meat, tea and cheese, and during 1941, jam and eggs were added.

On 23rd February 1942, one person was allowed 2oz tea; 6oz butter; 8 oz sugar; 4oz bacon; 3 oz cheese; 3 pints of milk; 2 oz fat and 1s 2d's (6p.'s) worth of meat each week. Jam was rationed at 1 lb and eggs at 3 per month.

With so many families in the town having back gardens and allotments, perhaps the shortage of food was not such a problem as in the big cities. In addition, of course, there was food in the countryside around the town. "There was always plenty of rabbits, stewed, baked or roasted" said David Grant. "We used to get them from friends and neighbours."

Ray Watkins tells a similar tale. "We used to catch rabbits during the war and no matter how you sneaked back into town, the bobby used to pop out of a doorway or somewhere...

'Where you been?' or 'Where you going?'

Ray's dad used to catch rabbits where he worked at Holton Heath and hang them in his raincoat.

'The bobby used to say, 'Open your raincoat!'

You used to open it, and two rabbits'd be hanging out!

He used to take one.

'You know you're not supposed to do this?' he'd say.'

I suppose it squared his conscience, and he'd let me go with the other one."

Ray told another story about food during the war, when Mr White at the fish shop had his delivery of salt fish. He was sent to get some.

"When we came out, we had a fight with the fish, trying to beat the hell out of each other with the fish. Mine flew off, and the tail came off. I tied it back on with a piece of string, and took it home.

I always remember the older of the two sisters said;-

'It's broken! I'm not having it like that!'

She marched me back down the fish shop, and she complained.

Mr. White said, it hadn't been dished out like that!. They'd been outside fighting!

Whereupon, he came out and shook the living daylights out of the schoolboy!

Clothes, furniture, and sweets were also rationed. The first was particularly hard on those teenaged girls who worked at Holton Heath and earned good wages. They now had money in their hands but nothing to spend it on. Some used to try to get the older men at the factory to sell them their unused coupons.

Petrol was virtually unobtainable, except for essential trades. Ken Ford reckoned these years were a busy time for his father who ran the Coventry House Garage at St. Martin's Pitch. By 1939, it was a thriving business. It had been started by Ken's grandfather, James Oliver, in the 1890s, for supplying cycles. The Fords were the agents for Sunbeam Cycles, hence the connection with Coventry. During the interwar years, more and more people were wanting bikes, and the business expanded. It also added petrol for the growing number of cars and lorries, as well as a garage for repairing them. Thus, it had done well.

Now with the coming of war, it faced serious problems. The government imposed restrictions on cars and on petrol, and there

Ray Watkins, 2002 [Author's collection]

was the prospect that its trade would be slashed, but Coventry House Garage became the only place in the town which was allowed to sell petrol. The army appropriated one pump, so there were always soldiers stopping by to fill up. The garage was also the only place where tyres, both for cars and for lorries could be obtained. The Fords used to have to buy them in bulk. "Hundreds and hundreds at a time... used to be falling out of the windows of the shop, there were so many in stock."(Ken Ford)

There were ways of getting round the petrol ban, as Ron Axon found after he left school when he used to spend his spare time driving his motorbike round the West Walls. This was just after the war when petrol was still rationed, but he would scrounge petrol coupons off old Mr. Hibbs. Ron recalled that petrol at this time was 1 shilling and 11Pence a gallon! (almost 10p.)

There were other more tangible signs that Britain was at war. Iron railings at the Almshouses were all cut down, together with those from private houses. Ostensibly this was to help with the war effort being turned into useful things for the military, but much of the iron was just piled in heaps, and according to Eddie Anderson, just left.

Jack Tubbs related that one morning — 1942, he thought — he saw an open lorry going to the churchyard with about four soldiers on boards and a German officer and a couple of coffins, which they then buried. "That was early in the morning, and I can always remember going there watching the remaining German doing a Nazi salute over the grave." There is nothing in Rodney Legg's *Dorset Aviation History* to identify the victims.

After Dunkirk the prospect of invasion was becoming very real. Marjorie Brewer was working in Poole in Bon Marche on the day after the evacuation.

"We girls had our hour for lunch and people kept coming into our shop and saying;- 'Lots of men down there (meaning on the Quay), and lots of people down there giving them chocolate and cigarettes.'

We girls all dashed down there, and there were all these men coming off the ships, all raggle-taggled ... beards... and looking all very weary, coming off the ships ... any ships, and it struck my mind –of course, I only had my lunch hour and I had to come on back, but we didn't know what had happened — but I've often thought since that there were all nationalities, all regiments, and if anyone had wanted to desert, then that was the time. They had no idea who the men were, which regiment they were from."

Marjorie has another memory of the effects of Dunkirk. Much later on, old Jack Kenway used to come into her pub when he was home on leave.

"He was sat in the little old tap room, having a pint, and the siren went, and old Jack was a great big bloke, and he shook like a leaf when he heard it. Her father said he had been at Dunkirk."

After Dunkirk, the threat of chemical warfare increased. Now everyone had to have a gasmask. For the government, the threat had always been there since September 1939, and right at the beginning gasmasks had been issued. "We always had to carry our gasmasks," recalled David Grant recently, "and we had practice in putting them on. They were issued in little cardboard boxes, but we used to get a tin cylinder lined with cloth and a tin lid with your name and address on the top." Once when Harold Rawles was cycling over to Ridge to see his grandparents, his gasmask got caught in his front wheel!

But for schoolchildren the war did have a pleasurable side. It opened up

The Town Hall. Notices on the wall, above the doorway, read "Buy Defence Bonds" and on the corner "British Restaurant". [Author's collection]

endless opportunities for amassing collections of trophies that were much more exciting than collecting cigarette cards or conkers. It could involve, for example, scouring the Common for trophies after a raid, looking for pieces of shrapnel, and taking them into school to show one's friends, gaining their admiration and envy. Most boys did this. As Ray Watkins sat in school one day, at his desk, he became aware of large pieces of shrapnel on the school roof. As soon as he was free, he and his friends got the gardening ladders and were up on the roof rescuing the treasures.

Later in the war, when incendiary bombs were dropped, he would cross the Common on his way to school to see if there were any fins from these bombs sticking out of the ground. If he found one, he would often try kicking the fin until he could pull it off, and then he would carry his new prize into school to show his friends. Harold Rawles was another avid collector of these treasures, so too was Ray Herridge. He often went armed with a coil of wire to attach to the fin to help him yank it out.

Sometimes in their enthusiasm to gain an important trophy, they would try something even more daring. "Being idiots," Ray admitted in recent years, "we took the fins off, and you could unscrew the bit at the end with a penny, and you could get the grey powder out – mix it with methylated spirits and it would burn through a plate! Some (bombs) were filled with black ends, which were even more explosive, and they were fastened on with a band of black sticky tape. We were daft enough to take them off the ends!" In this way, he got to know that German bombs and English ones were different. English ones had a strip of cordite at the end and not the black ends as the German ones had. Yet, as Ray concedes now, in spite of the foolhardiness of what they were doing, "none of us got hurt!"

Ron admitted searching for bullets, even digging them up if necessary. He then removed their black powder, if it was a German bullet, or the cordite, if it were English, and tried to explode it! "You'd get a terrific flash for a few seconds. Then you'd get the next bullet!"

Perspex from crashed aircraft, or any other bit of such a plane, was another prize to be gained. Ray Herridge recalled picking up bits of the white rubber that surrounded the petrol tank. "If a bullet went in, the rubber would seal itself up again. One boy brought in lots of bits. If you poked a hole in it, it did re-seal."

When they heard of any plane coming down, boys were eager to go and search it. "We'd go all over the place when planes did crash," confessed Ron. Once he kept on to his father so much about one that had come down at the bottom of Creech Barrow, on the Creech Road at Aldermoor. "I kept on for him to take me, and he did, on the bar of his bike."

Radio jamming rings were also things to be sought after. "They looked a bit like Christmas decorations," thought Harold Rawles.

Naturally, everything had to be taken in to school to show to one's friends and rivals. A piece of this "marvellous stuff" made them envious and improved one's status. One boy came in once with a bit of a German newspaper that he had picked up. He had, no doubt, got to the plane before the authorities, as did Eddie Anderson that day he cycled down to Arne, as he did every day delivering newspapers. That day was different. When he returned home he was carrying a pilot's boot. His mother was far from pleased. She was horrified and made him throw it away. She had noticed flesh still inside the boot!

It was reckoned that boys living out on the coast had a greater opportunity for amassing trophies. They used to come in with all sorts of bits and pieces from planes that had come down. One boy from Kimmeridge, Ray recalled, came in one day with a live shell, and was seen at dinnertime tapping the thing! On another occasion, some one even brought in a personnel bomb. They used to open out like a flower.

No wonder the Head Master at the big school called for an amnesty by urging his pupils to bring in all their ammunition and their bits of German planes to see who had the biggest collection. When the boys did so, there was a "bloke all dressed up in a funny suit, like Dan Dare, and he had big boxes to put the stuff in." (Ray H.)

Ray Herridge talked about another adventure he and his friends got up to. "We had loads of aeroplanes down here. They used to park them outside the old police station on a lorry called the *Queen Mary*. We used to go round to the Police Station side, because the people were in Burgess's Café (in South Street) having tea, and we used to bend off bits of the plane. I remember bending off a bit with a little cross on it. When I bent it off, a voice says;-

'You'll be not going to do anything with that, are you?'

And the old inspector came out and took it into the Police Station."

Gradually all the young men in the town were called up. Archie Brennan was among those who volunteered at the outset of the war. In 1939, he was working as a gardener for Mr. Churchill, when his employer suddenly died. Since Archie was then too near military age no one would give him a permanent job. This was frustrating, so he went up to Southampton and volunteered. That was on the Tuesday. On Friday, he was in the army, and his army service saw him with the fighting in the deserts of North Africa, as a Desert Rat.

It was much later on that Harold Rawles came of an age to be called-up. He was able to go where he wanted, into the RAF. His mum, like many other mothers up and down the country, was very upset. He suspected that his dad was as well, but he did not show it, but "my dad wouldn't shut or lock the door when I went, just in case I came home unexpected like." Of the 28 shillings (£1.40p.) a week he was paid, he sent his mother one pound. "She put it away in a club book and didn't use it at all."

For most of his service he was stationed at Hixon Airfield in Staffordshire. This was a holding station for vehicles – some 4500 at any one time. "We had the job, six of us, of servicing the vehicles before they were dispatched to other units." At the very end of the war, he did volunteer to go to Kenya and even went up to Warrington for training, but the authorities decided that as he only had nine or ten months to do before he was demobbed, it was not worth sending him, so

Archie Brennan, taken in Italy.
[Archie Brennan]

he never went.

It was the RAF, too, for Tom Newberry and Vic Lillington. Vic joined as an apprentice after passing the examination when he was 16 ½. After three years training, he saw experience in Egypt and the Sudan as well as in this country. He and his fellow engineers were trained with jeeps, motorbikes, cycles and fixed guns which were to be dropped from the air from Lancaster bombers.

Jack Tubbs was another airman. He joined up in 1941, and found himself attached to the Airborne Division, which prepared supplies and dropped them wherever they were needed. Jeeps, motorbikes, bicycles and field guns were all assembled and packed into converted Halifax bombers. "Very often they needed a hammer to release them. They were dropped on four 60 foot parachutes. They had a hydraulic system on board the planes. There were two mushroom rods down the side of each crate. They were attached to a central shackle, hydraulically controlled. The theory was when the mushroom rods hit the deck, the centre shackle was released, and the four 'shutes sailed away. When it landed, it was just the case of pulling off the metal boost from the top and driving it away. Very, very often, it wouldn't work that way. It wouldn't release in mid-air!"

Jack, Vic, and Harold were fortunate. They were able to go where they wanted. Far less fortunate was Ray Watkins. When he received his calling-up papers, he found they had stuck him in the mines, the last thing that he wanted! What he and most boys all wanted was to get into one of the fighting services, where all the excitement was, or so they thought. They had little concept of the horrors of war and regarded the mines as a soft option.

When he heard where he was to be sent,

First pupil of Swanage Grammar School to become one of Lord Trenchard's "Brats", RAF Halton apprentice, Vic Lillington [Vic Lillington]

Vic Lillington in a Gloster Gladiator of 80 Squadron, 1939. He left England to go to Egypt with the Squadron the year before. [Vic Lillington]

Ray was devastated, since he was well experienced in the local school cadets and highly thought of as a good future soldier by his officers in Wareham. So, Ray made an official objection, which was supported by his Headmaster Mr. Stuckley, who ran the corps. He protested saying 'What is the use of forming army cadets if the army is going to put them in the mines?'

Ray was called to Southampton, to a hearing. About ten other young men were there as well. The chairman of the board asked him his name and if he had requested not to go in the mines.

"I said, 'Yes, sir!'

'Oh? Your request has been refused,' he said, without any discussion or explanation!"

Such treatment was not an isolated affair, for some of Ray's other friends in the army cadets were also sent to the mines. Thus, Ray became a Bevin Boy[1], and was sent up to County Durham on 18th September 1944, to Annfield Plain, two miles from Stanley. He was given a month's training and then two weeks on the surface before going underground. He lived in a hostel for 400 to 500 boys. He was far from happy, and only put up with this for about six months. Mainly, he found it difficult to live on the £3 a week he was paid. "Ten shillings (50p.) for

Income Tax; then, deductions for pit head baths, which they hadn't got. The hostel gave only two meals, so you had to buy food. I found I was sending home to mother for money. Board was 30 shillings (£1.50p.)." He could not live on this. Lonely, homesick and exhausted, he did think of absconding, but was lucky in finding lodgings, with a Mr. and Mrs Travers. Their son had just got married and had moved out, so they had a space for Ray. He enjoyed being there.

Ray Watkins, taken after his last shift, 1947 at Cragshead, County Durham. [Ray Watkins]

These five men are only just a handful of the many who were called-up, and, as such, they are only a representative selection. There were, of course, others who for medical reasons, or because they were in a protected occupation could not join the services. Herbie Elmes was one of these latter. At this time he was working in the cordite factory at Holton Heath. He was certainly keen to do his bit and was not prepared to wait until he was called-up. With his friend, Jimmy Benjafield, he went to see the Superintendent.

"We'd like to join up.'

'If you want to be foolish,' he said,' you can. If you sever connection with Holton Heath, there's no superannuation. You'll lose that. If you wait till you're called, when you get a rise here, your money will be made up. If you, chaps, go, we shall have to put in others, but you are trained, been here for years. If you want to go, go, but I think you're very foolish.'

So we thought it over and decided to wait." And being at Holton Heath, Herbie was never called-up. He was regarded as a keyworker.

As far as many of the men still left in the town were concerned, there was only one question on their lips. That was "Where is the beer?" The lack of it certainly showed Britain was a country under siege. Pubs were only allowed a certain amount of drink, and once that was used up, they could get no more until supplies were resumed. Scotch was particular difficult to get, and once that was used up, publicans did not know when they would get the next supply. Therefore, hours of opening became heavily restricted.

It was no good a pub opening if it had no beer. Often, it meant just two days a week trading.

Even when supplies did come in, the locals regarded the beer as being very watered down, and the price had trebled. Just before the war, it was 6d a pint (2 1/2p.), but early in the war, it has risen to 1 shilling and 3 pence (just over 6p.)

The shortage of glasses was equally worrying for landlords. "We couldn't get them," commented Marjorie Brewer. "The ones we could get were like jam jars! Of course, you had to keep an eye on them, or else they'd disappear. Customers wouldn't let go of them. If they didn't have a glass, they wouldn't get another pint."

Landlords used to watch each other to see if they could make their supply of beer stretch further.

"Go and see what time Yorkie Yates (the landlord of the *Duke of Wellington*) is going to open." Her father used to say. "Let him have first go." He would then have to deal with the queue that would form outside, and his ration would soon be consumed, leaving the Brewers to make their share of drink last all evening.

Wareham, like most towns, had its British Restaurant. These were opened at the government's insistence, to provide good hot meals at a very low cost, so that everyone could have one good meal a day. That for Wareham was at the Granary, which was redesigned to the purpose, having a few years before been where the fire engine was stored. The work was carried by the local building firm of A.T. Moss, and Jack Spiller made most of the new windows for it. When it was ready in 1942, the *Dorset County Chronicle* announced that meals –three course – cost only 6d (2 1/2p.) for children and 8d (3 1/2p.) for adults. Eddie Anderson was a frequent diner there, because his mother received tickets for the family's school lunches there. He still remembers how good the meals were. He also added, "All the children made a row, so they decided to get a woman up there reading from a book! That was the worse thing they could have done. All the children wanted was a hot meal." The canteen also supplied dinners to Pinkie Skewes' school in North Street.

Another area the war opened up was in entertainment with the idea of keeping the nation's morale high. Herbie Elmes' records show he was in great demand during the war years as a comic magician; for example, in 1943, he was at the Senior School in Wareham, the Empire in Hamworthy, the Drill Hall in Wimborne, at Holton Heath, at Poole, at the Great Hall in Parkstone, at Wool, Sandford, at Upton Village Hall, Lytchett, East Creech at the Wareham Fire Brigade's Christmas Party, at Morden with the Young Farmers' Club, Stoborough and at Moreton .

The Old Granary Tea House became the British Restaurant.
[Author's collection]

In addition, the town had a Utility Band, under Bobby Green as conductor. Miss Bradford played the accordion. She, Herbie described, as the only one who could actually play an instrument. Perhaps he was being hyper-critical, but it does highlight the fact that the musicians were playing because they enjoyed doing so, and helping to keep their audiences happy, which help to boost morale. Jack Spiller played trumpet in the band, Frankie Adams his banjo, Harry Bradford the Swanee River Whistle Mouthorgan, L. Street the drums, J. Lay the trombone, H. Barter the violin and Herbie himself the bass. The band were in great demand playing popular music at concerts and dances all over Dorset and Hampshire.

At Holton Heath, the workers used to put on their own entertainment, bright variety shows for the benefit of their fellow workers. This was typical of large factories at this time, giving their workers opportunities for using their talents for the benefit of their colleagues. At the cordite factory, on a Wednesday evening in 1944 the workers organised a concert for the Wings For Victory campaign. Among those who took part was Pam James, who was then 11. She performed a tap dance with her mother who worked in the factory. Then there were I. McElvie a light comedian, G. Dunbarton , a bass-baritone, D. Steele with his character sketches, K. Dance, a contralto and R. Abbott, a tenor. Herbie Elmes was there, too, doing his conjuring tricks. Such entertainment was, of course, designed to keep up the morale of the workers, as was the radio programme *Workers' Play Time,* a regular variety show which came from a factory "somewhere in England," but the girls at Holton were not allowed the radio on. Their work needed their full concentration.

The war brought personal problems. When a young soldier, or a girl, did find someone he, or she, wanted to get to know better, being at war did not make for an easy time. Most couples had to be content with a few hours together snatched when the boyfriend came home on leave. That was bad enough, but Vic Lillington found even more problems. His girl worked at Bletchley in Buckinghamshire, the high security place. It was, she said, "a marvellous place, with beautiful grounds.

Not that we saw much of that." Her duty involved two days, from 8 till 4; then, two evenings, 4 till midnight, followed by two nights, midnight till 8.0 am; then, a forty-eight hour stand-off.

Fitting their courtship in between Audrey's hours off and his leave, was extremely difficult. "I used to rush off to Nottingham to see Vic, or he'd come down and see me when it was my stand-off. He used to spend the night on Rugby Station!"

Her future husband recalled one special evening's difficulties. "She came up to Nottingham to see me on her twenty-first birthday, and I waited and waited on the station. The trains were all over the place." The reason for the delay, Audrey explained; "We shunted! Go from Bletchley to Bedford. Change there

Audrey Frost - Women's Royal Auxiliary Air Force (c1940-45).

and get on the other station, and go up through Market Harborough. It shunted this way and it shunted that way, and got into Nottingham station at midnight."

Then their problems were not over. "I'd booked (a room for the night) in the YMCA, because this was before we were married, and we rushed down to the YM, and hammered on the door.

The woman in charge said, 'Good Heavens! You're late!'

I said, 'Well, it's the trains!,'"

Having only just met her intended, Audrey did not want to have to say 'Goodnight' and leave him on the doorstep, so she pleaded, 'Can I just say 'Goodnight'?'

'Yes,' she said, 'Five minutes!'

And that was my twenty-first birthday!"

Whenever they met hurriedly like this, on a railway station, Audrey used to get back to Bletchley, "so tired," worn out with so much travelling. If Vic was able to accompany her back to Bletchley, he then faced the prospect of a wait on that station. "Three trains went through before Vic's. No where to go in Bletchley … a dead place. One person did take pity on us and offered us a cup of tea; that was after we were married."

Their difficulties were certainly not unique. Every courting couple faced severe problems during the war. If a couple decided to get married, then war brought further difficulties. Often weddings were either postponed until the war was over, or they were hastily arranged when the bridegroom had, say, forty-eight hours leave.

Joan Anderson's to Jim Brien in 1941 was typical. A prospective bride could not expect a white wedding. To have one was too expensive. A white dress was extremely difficult to get since all clothes were rationed. The only way round this would have been to save up and buy the material and make it herself, or get a friend to do it. Most girls found this impossible, so they did without. Joan did manage to save up enough (money and coupons) for a new coat and a new hat, but she also had to do without the traditional wedding service in church. With food rationing on, there was no chance of getting the traditional cake, and a honeymoon was also out. "During the war, you accepted it. You couldn't get the fruit. Instead, we had paste sandwiches" Afterwards, she continued to live with her mother. Houses were scarce.

After all their difficulties in their courtship, Vic Lillington and Audrey did make it, and were able to have a much more traditional day. Their marriage did place in church, albeit a tiny little one, and in Essex, where Audrey came from. She did have a special outfit, though not a traditional wedding dress. "Didn't do things like that, wear white, in wartime!" That she was able to have a new suit was due to her father being a costumier in London, whose premises was at the back of Peter Robinson's. They were also able to have a honeymoon in Torquay, setting off on the train at 3.0 and not arriving at their destination until midnight.

Vic Lillington in Aquir, Palestine at the end of the war. [Vic Lillington]

By 1941 Ernest Bevin, the Minister for Labour, had wide powers over people's employment.

Chapter 6
War Work.

Never before had there been such a demand for workers. The needs of war were urgent, and the government responded. On 10 March 1941 the *Daily Express* carried as its headline; ' 100,000 Women Wanted in Two Weeks'. Ernest Bevin, the Minister for Labour, had begun using his powers to recruit more women for essential services. From now on all single women, aged between 20 and 30, were to be employed in the auxiliary services or in munitions. The only exceptions were those in fulltime education or study, and those with domestic responsibilities. Consequently, the lives of a majority of young women were completely changed and Wareham was no exception in this respect.

Most of the local girls did their war work at Holton Heath, but it was not only Wareham girls who worked there. They came from a wide area, even as far as Poole and Parkstone. Holton Heath was the Royal Naval cordite factory which made explosives, packing it into bombs and shells – the 'tools' that the armed services depended upon. In fact, Holton Heath was vital to the war effort.

Since production had to go on virtually non-stop, all the staff worked in shifts. The early one started at 6 o'clock in the morning and finished at 2 in the afternoon, the second shift took over until 10 o'clock at night. Then the third shift ran from 11.0pm all through the night until 6 the next day. "About 3 o'clock in the morning we used to have a break and I used to have a cooked dinner. There was a very good canteen there." (Marjorie) These shifts were worked in a rota for a week each.

The worst shift, reckoned Marjorie Brewer, was the second. "It was a rotten shift! One week in three I couldn't go out to a dance. From that 10 shift we didn't get home till 11." In addition, if the girls did that shift on a Saturday as well, which they did at one time for several months, things worked out even worse. "We would get home at 11 o'clock on Saturday night; then, up at 5 on Monday, ready for the early shift again….(but) it was an experience. You were young and you could do it!"

Doris Fooks joined the working force at the age of seventeen. She had wanted to go into the RAF but that was not possible, so it was across to Holton Heath for her. For all the staff from Wareham the early shift meant being at the station to catch the train at a quarter to six in the morning. "We had a special train that used to pick us up at Wareham Station. They used to call it 'The Glamour Express'. 5d

The uniform which had to be worn at Holton Heath in the danger area. It had been designed by a Miss Cross and Mrs E Wills, (nee Churchill), after the horrific accident to Miss Nora Bishop who was badly burnt but survived in 1929. Up to then the girls had worn dresses. This photograph was taken soon after the uniform was introduced - dark blue serge with a pale blue collar and special felt soled shoes. [Author's collection]

(2p) return to Holton Heath. All us girls were in our teens. Sometimes, it forgot to turn up because the engine driver had overslept and the alarm hadn't gone off."(Marjorie) At the start of the war, when Doris James first went, the girls had to catch a bus which picked up from the *Red Lion*.

Dolly and Kath Fry used to cycle in every day from Furzebrook, leaving their bikes at Wareham Station. From there they continued by train.

Girls who needed breakfast carried it in a small case and the canteen staff would cook it for them.

Rules were strictly enforced. On arriving at the factory there was a random search as they passed through. No metal was allowed at all. No suspenders! Only a gold wedding ring was acceptable. Any other metal which had been brought in had to be surrendered as it might react with the explosives. Cigarette lighters were also taboo and had to be left at the gate. Then, the girls had to change into their uniforms; fire-proofed clothes, "horrible serge navy trousers," in Doris's words, "shapeless tunics and a covering for the hair." Hair grips were not allowed and every end of hair had to be tucked up. Then, the girls had another search before going into the danger zone.

Moreover, it was highly dangerous work. Doris' job was in the paper room, where big rolls were fed into a cutting machine before being dipped into nitro-glycerine and left to pulp for four hours. Supervising the girls were those who wore a red spot on their sleeves, while over them were those with blue spots. When either was around the girls all knew they had to behave but on balance, Doris feels, the work was "good fun." A sentiment echoed by Marjorie; "I had a lot of fun" she reminisced. It was a "wonderful" experience she would not have wanted to miss. "All the girls got on ever so well."

She was in the press room – the 'cheese room' – with four or five other girls. Electric trucks brought the cordite up to one of the six press houses. The trucks were heated to keep the cordite warm. "It came up to us in slices, like sliced bread, and we used to put them in a press, pull the lever down and press them. They used to come out like a solid block and the truck driver'd take them off to another place."

"It could be bitterly cold," as the only heat in the factory, Marjorie recalled, was in the electric trucks. "One woman announced one day that she had her husband's long johns under her trousers."

Marjorie was very relieved that she was never assigned to the Roller Houses. "I never went down there, but they were always having fires down there, and men used to get burned badly; terrible, frightening really. I was scared to death that they were going to put me down there. You had to do what you were told."

Nor did she ever work in the Teryl department. Teryl was a pale yellow crystalline material that was widely used in bombs and shells, wrote Malcolm Bowditch and Les Hayward in their book, *A Pictorial Record of the Royal Naval Cordite Factory, Holton Heath,* 1996. "Girls could get more money working here, but it used to turn them yellow!" (Marjorie)

One great asset for young women working at Holton Heath was a social one. It provided Doris, for example, with many more companions than she had had at Hicks'. "We all got on alright." To get the best out of the staff, girls were allowed, for certain reasons, to have time off. "My boyfriend's coming home on a week's leave," girls would tell the foreman. "I want a week off," and it was usually allowed. It was one way of keeping morale high.

Another incentive was high pay —£3 a week. It was certainly better than shopwork which had been only 10 shillings (50p) a week for Doris at Hicks'. This was much more than Marjorie had in her pocket every week, for although she received the same amount at Bon Marche, a quarter of that went on her trainfare to Poole. "When I went to Holton Heath and in my first wage packet there was over £3 in it,…my goodness!… I was a millionaire!" The extra money gave both girls much more independence and more to spend on clothes, though as Marjorie admitted, "you couldn't go out anywhere. You couldn't buy make-up. There wasn't any. If there was, there'd be a queue a mile long!"

A further incentive at Holton was that girls felt they were doing their bit for the war. "Someone had to keep the factories going, didn't they?"

June Thompson managed to get released from her job in the civil service at Portsmouth when her father was promoted to take over at Holton Heath. She was able to get transferred to the cash office, where she did the salaries and wages for the workers. At the time she was nineteen.

"On Fridays," she recalled, "we used to have to go down to the other part of the factory – to the main gate – and pay all the workers as they came off their shifts. We started on Mondays calculating their wages for the previous week and it took us right up through till when we actually laid up the wages. In Portsmouth there were 28,000 workers. At Holton Heath there were a large number of people, but it was a small office, so I got to know everyone.

We came into the bank at Wareham, and were accompanied by a policeman with a gun when we carried the money back."

June's family lived on the site, in a house overlooking the main gate.

"There was a gate across the road. No traffic lights then. A little shop. Mr and Mrs Groves used to run it, with a couple of petrol pumps at their shop, which was really the front room of their bungalow. Sold everything from shoelaces to a pound of lard… anything.

The road to Poole was closed. A sentry at either side, and no one was allowed to go along that road. The only people who could were the ones with passes. I used to look out the bedroom window and see the sentry on duty with his rifle."

With German U-boats patrolling the Atlantic, food from the Commonwealth and from America was cut off, so it was vital for Britain to raise as much food as possible from her own soil. Hence the drive for householders to grow their own in the *Dig for Victory* Campaign, and, with many agricultural men in the services, the drive to recruit girls to help with farming; the result…. landgirls.

In 1941 there were 20,000 landgirls but three years later their numbers had quadrupled to 80,000. After an initial training period of four weeks, when the girls received £1.40p a week, they were sent out to work a 50 hour week. During harvest periods their hours were much longer. As trained personnel they earned

£2.40 a week but out of this had to come £1.25 a week for their lodgings. However, they could have seven days holiday with pay each year.

It had been during the First World War that the Women's Land Army had been set up, organised by Lady Gertrude Denham. In 1938, as war approached, this was re-organised, again with Lady Gertrude in control.

Like many other rural areas, Wareham had its influx of landgirls. One of those who came was Lois Howe, now Mrs. Hibberd. Before the war she "lived in a pretty part of Cheam in Surrey and I always had a great love of the country, so it seemed an opportunity to enrole as a landgirl rather than in the forces. Looking back, I must have seemed an unlikely candidate for heavy work on a farm, as I was anything but big and brawny, but my success at maths at school led the interviewer to suggest I joined the Timber Corps. So after a short training period with the Forestry Commission at Lydney in Gloucestershire, I qualified as a timber measurer."

This Women's Timber Corps formed part of the WLA. and had been set up by the Home Grown Timber Department of the Ministry of Supply in 1942. Lois was sent to Wareham, where she was given lodgings with Mr. and Mrs. Watkins and their son, Ray. "I remember them with great affection as they were so kind to me. I stayed with them for about three years." Here she found herself billetted with another landgirl, Daphne Handley-Bird.

The two girls were sent to the sawmills, "a short cycle ride away. We worked from a small log hut with a tortoise stove in the centre, which we lit every morning and it gave a good heat, boiling a kettle or milk for cocoa on top. I also recall bright yellow saffron buns we bought, a speciality of the café near the station (Hibbs's?) .

Our job was to measure

L-R Lois Howe, Pearl ?, Gwen Pond: at Cranmore Sawmill c.1942 [Lois Howe]

the timber cut down as the men were paid on the amount produced. We also had to calculate the volume of timber, with the aid of a mathematical table called a 'Hoppus Measurer,' as it was off-loaded from the timber lorries. The saw-mill produced railway sleepers and pit props for the mines on a long bench equipped with a large circular saw. This was a fearsome machine, but I can only remember one serious accident when a man lost his thumb.

Some of our work took us into the forests and big country estates to measure beautiful Scots Pines, Wellingtonias and other great trees when they were felled as part of the war effort. I felt so sad for the owners – sometimes they were looking out of their windows when another giant tree was felled and the tractors dragged it off down the drive.

I was later transferred to another small mill at Moreton, but I was still able to travel to and from Wareham with a railway warrant."

Lois also found herself recruited as an ambulance driver by the St. John's Brigade. "To qualify, I had to drive the entire team at night with blacked out headlights, wearing a gasmask over my glasses which became steamed up so I couldn't see a thing! Thankfully we all arrived safely at the nearest pub!"

Win was another Land-girl, who lodged for a time at Percy and Bet Best's. Percy referred to her as "a strapping girl" who was in charge of the Italian Prisoners of War, dredging weeds out of the river the town side of Baggs' mill. When she was once asked if the Italians tried anything on, she replied, "They hadn't better!" After the War Win moved away and the Bests lost touch with her.

Teenager Harold Rawles had the job of ferrying some of the landgirls round. He picked some up from Wareham Station, some from Wimborne and others from Bere Regis and then he would take them off to the places where they worked. At night he would be round for them again to ferry them back. It could be a sweaty, sensuous experience for an eighteen year old, he recently recalled. "One of the girls would sit aside the gearstick and I used to change gear quite often!"

Phyl Marsh became involved in another kind of war work, helping to run the WVS canteen on the Quay. She did a duty twice a week, on a Tuesday and a Friday, working from two o'clock in the afternoon until ten at night. This facility was invaluable, hot meals were provided as well as sandwiches and cakes. The latter could be as cheap as 1d (1/2p.). Phyl was usually on the sandwich counter. In this work, as in other spheres, the social classes were well and truly mixed. Helping out when it was her turn was Lady Drax of Charlborough Park. She did not particularly enjoy serving customers, so she opted to stay in the kitchen and wash up. She was good to Phyl as "she often used to come and pick me up." Lady Lees of Lytchett was another energetic worker, as was Mrs Moss, the wife of Moss the town's leading builder and one-time mayor. Ray Herridge described her as "a dapper little lady who used to dress like Queen Mary".

Her friend, Renee Burt, often persuaded Phyl to help out with the ambulance. The first time she did this Phyl had to be enrolled. Mrs Bond of Tyneham House came and performed the ceremony.

On one occasion George Henson, Wareham's Registrar of Births and Deaths, approached her, as she was a good friend of his wife, and asked her to go with him in the ambulance to take a woman to Herrison Hospital near Dorchester, which at that time specialised in mental illness. He had found a poor old woman wandering around Wareham in her nightie. She had no idea where she was. "She couldn't remember anything. She was crying. Although she was alright, I put my hand over the back of the seat and she hung on to it. When we got down there and I had to leave her, she hung on and screamed." Phyl also helped him take a lady who was expecting a baby imminently. The problem was that they had to go first to Dorchester to take the lady's daughter there so she would be looked after, and then come back to Wimborne before the birth. "Of course, it was getting near and the roads were all bumpy. George said to me;-

'You sure you're alright?'

I said, 'Yes. Alright! But get there quickly!'".

They did so, without the baby arriving first, much to the relief of Phyl and her driver.

Even men at home were ordered to do more for the war if they were in occupations deemed as not essential for the war. Ted Brewer as a landlord of a pub was told that with the war on he should be doing an additional job – "a wartime job." As a result he became a baker's roundsman for the Co-op. However the first time he went out it was nearly a disaster, as his daughter recalled,

"I'd got back from work and asked where father was?

'I don't know where he's got to. He went out with that bread van and he's not back yet!'

He did come back exclaiming, 'Talk about a part time job, mother! Look at the time it's taken!"

And no wonder! Without knowing the route it was very difficult to find his way, especially when it grew dark. His van had no lights and the blackout made it even worse. "He had to go ever so carefully all the way back."

But in spite of this experience, he did grow to like the job. He loved horses, explained his daughter, and he developed quite a rapport with Bob, as the horse was called. Once, when he arrived at the Co-op for work the manager told him that they had used up all the horse-feed and new supplies from Bournemouth had not yet been delivered. Yet the manager still required Bob to take the bread round. Ted refused.

"Have you had your breakfast, yet?' he asked.

'Of course, I have!'

'Well, I don't go out until that horse had has his! So, you'd better get onto Bournemouth!'"

Chapter 7
The Raid of 16th December 1942, and others.

Wareham received only one raid, and, compared with the regular hammering of Coventry, Southampton and Plymouth, even this incident can hardly be described as major, but for the townsfolk at the time it did seem very serious indeed with several houses destroyed and four deaths.

The quiet streets of the town seemingly unprepared for the raid in December 1942. North Street, with St. Martin's Church in the background. [Author's collection]

It all happened on December 16th 1942, which was a Wednesday, when a German plane — a Dornier 217 — flew low over the town — 500 feet up, according to the *Dorset County Chronicle* — and dropped several bombs. It would appear that it was not part of some big sortie on the town, or the aftermath of one when the enemy planes were trying to dump their remaining bombs to lighten their passage across the Channel. Rather it was a lone flier. Rodney Legg in *Dorset's War, 1939 - 1945* records that a single aircraft on the same day at lunchtime dropped bombs on Poole Quay. Perhaps the attacker on Wareham was the same pilot.

The raid on the town happened suddenly. The plane just slipped in under the radar at Worth Matravers, so there was no siren and no warning. People were just getting on with their work.

David Grant was at the post office in North Street working as a messenger boy. He had now left school. His job was to deliver telegrams and anything else around the town, and between jobs he lent a hand anywhere it was needed. Just before noon on that Wednesday he was helping George Ballard, the general factotum of the post office, to move some extra pigeon holes across the yard from the garage behind the post office. It was coming up to Christmas and more sorting boxes were needed for the anticipated great rush of greetings cards.

Further up North Street, Miss Bussell's sweet shop had just closed for its lunch hour and Dan'l Coombes, the errand boy there, was on his way home, while his employer turned to get her own meal.

At the *Lord Nelson*, Mrs Inie Ash was out-at-the-back, just about to dish up the nice rabbit stew that she had made earlier. She was waiting. It would not be long before her youngest daughter, Peggy, came in. It was her half-day, and at this moment she was probably on the train that was heading towards the station.

At the new senior school, Ray Herridge was crossing the playground, and in Bennett's shop in East Street, Ray Watkins was busy just finishing a little job that he wanted to get done before he scooted off home for his lunch. The rest of the workers had gone and the shop was now empty and quiet as he made his way through the deserted premises and out of the back door. As he had to pass the bakehouse on his way into the lane he paused to exchange a few words with Mr. Lee, the confectioner. That done he turned to step into the lane.

Down at the far end of South Street Beryl Binding, who had not long left school, was tidying up at World Stores, one of the town's busy groceries. She was stacking up the empty cardboard boxes at the rear of the shop under the tin roof which covered the yard. As it was Wednesday afternoon, the early closing day, she would soon be home.

Her sister, Win, was already there in Nundico sitting in a chair in the living room. From here she had a good view over the Purbeck Hills. Nearby, Mrs Win Axon was standing at the door, waiting no doubt for her son, Ron, to come for his lunch.

Phyl Marsh was at home up the Sandford Road. She was in a quandary. Her friend who should have been doing an afternoon shift down at the WVS on the Quay, had asked Phyl if she would mind changing with her and doing her duty this Wednesday, which Phyl had readily agreed to. The only problem was that she could not now remember whether she had to be there at two o'clock or half past. After a lot of debating with herself, she told her mother that she would go down for 2.15. In that way, she said, she could apologise either for being late, or for being early.

Marjorie Brewer at Holton Heath was conscious that it was another couple of hours before she finished. She was on the early shift this week and that did not end until 2 o'clock. Still she hoped those two hours would go quickly.

Suddenly, Dan'l, David, Beryl and Ray in Wareham, were each aware of a low flying aeroplane. They assumed it was an English one, although Ray was puzzled as to why it was so low. It seemed to be following South Street. David stopped halfway across the post office yard, Dan'l was halfway home, and Ray was in the bakehouse garden. To Win, because it was so low, it seemed like a big flying boat. Beryl had turned and was walking back into the shop. Then, machine gun firing stopped her dead in her tracks.

"I looked round, but I couldn't see it," Ray later recalled. "The next thing, it opened fire!"

Nearby, one of its bullets went clean though the

The alleyway at the back of Bennett's Bakery in East Street. The Bakehouse on the left, with the stables for the horse just off out of site to the left. [Ray Watkins]

papers that a young clerk was working on. She was injured, though the *Dorset Country Chronicle* reporter was not certain whether this was the result of the bullet or from flying glass.

The noise of the plane spurred Dan'l into action. He raced home, knowing his mother was alone in the house. "We're going to get bombed!" she yelled in fear when she saw her son. Thinking that they could not possibly reach the safety of the garden shelter in time, Dan'l yanked open the toilet door and pushed his mother inside and then squeezed in himself. There they remained until it grew quiet again.

The put-put of the machine gun galvinised Beryl into action. She dived in among the cider crates for safety and cowered there. Mr. Beck, the manager, yelled "You silly fool. Come on in here!" With that he yanked her in his office and pushed her under his desk.

Her sister, in her chair in Nundico, had a good view of the approaching plane. She could see the bombs coming out and was frozen in horror.

Once they had got over their shock, David and old George made a bolt for the post office as fast as they could.

Likewise, after a moment of sheer terror, Ray turned and fled back to the bakehouse. "Mr. Lee," he yelled, "I've just seen a plane dropping bombs ! It can't be far away!"

"The station?" came a reply.

"No, nearer than that!"

Gingerly, Ray crept into the lane and a few minutes later out into North Street. What he saw has stayed with him ever since. It was a mass of glass, tiles and bits of wood, strewn haphazardly about. "The further up North Street I went I was convinced the bombs were in the street." When he got closer to St. Martin's he could see Bussell's shop. Its windows were all blown out. "God!" he thought, "It must have dropped there!" All over the street he could see the contents of its once well stocked shelves that had filled the windows; sweets, flour, treacle, jars and boxes all littering the street. Inside, absolutely everything had been blown off its crowded shelves.

"There were bits of chimney pots, slates and so forth, all over the place," added Ray Herridge. He had come home for lunch the backway, down by Christmas Close and along the Walls. "Wood and rubbish lying about all over the place, and we were told to Scram!"

But Ray Watkins' original diagnosis was wrong. None of the bombs had fallen on Bussell's shop. On the contrary, one had come down across the road in a garden on Mount Pleasant, at the back of the *Lord Nelson,* and had ricocheted off some wire netting that was buried in the earth there. Then it had flown past the *Nelson*, where Mrs. Ash was just about to dish up. Looking up, she was utterly amazed by what she then saw. Not only was a German plane flying past her windows but inside she had a clear view of the pilot. Then the machine disappeared from her sight, leaving its bomb to come down on the gasworks where it started a fire, fortunately a small one. A second bomb had pitched on the riverbank, carving out a huge hole as it fell, and breaking the legs of a goat that was on the riverside, while a third one landed in the watermeadows, and as far as Ken Ford knows, or anyone else for that matter, it is still there today! Because of where they fell, Maurie Ash was convinced that it was the station that was the intended target, but the pilot had misjudged the distance and had released his bombs too early.

The train, which had been approaching the station, came to a sudden halt some distance away. On board, Maurie's daughter had heard the noise of the plane and the bombs falling and she was now very alarmed, fearing for the safety of her parents.

Unfortunately, there was a fourth bomb. This was the one that had landed across the road from Miss Bussell's, at the back of three cottages there and had demolished the drill hall. It was the one that had done the most damage, and had seriously injured both Harry Bradford, the collector for the Liverpool Victoria Insurance Company, and his next-door neighbour, E. Fry, the painter and decorator. Both were rushed off to hospital. The third home to be damaged by this bomb belonged to the headmaster of the West Street School, and later young Ray Herridge took schoolboy delight in the damage caused to his headmaster's house. It was "blown to smithereens!"

But before this, at midday, Mrs Watkins was waiting for her son to come home for his lunch when the bombs had fallen. He found his mother at the bottom of Shatter's Hill, worried about him.

"You alright?" she asked.

"Yes," he reassured her.

"I was worried about you. I knew you'd be coming home from work about this time."

Ray asked about his home.

"Windows have all been blown out and the door won't shut."

A lot of other houses in the town had been similarly affected. Ray Herridge remembered "the reed ceiling of the back room (where he lived) had fallen down. It fell into the stew. We still had to eat it, but we hooked the lumps of plaster out with a spoon!"

When Beryl and the staff at World Stores emerged from their hiding places the interior of the shop was in chaos. Everything had fallen off shelves. There was coffee, that was a luxury item, all over the floor. Beryl herself was still frightened. "I wouldn't go home. My mum knew I wouldn't come home. My brother came down and got me when the 'all-clear' went."

By this time Dan'l felt it was safe enough for him to return to the chaos of Bussell's, where he found his elderly employer very much alive. Seeing him, she resolutely declared "Come on! We've got work to do!" and without more words she and her errand boy set to with brushes and brooms sweeping up all the mess from the floor and from the street. They tipped most of it into the dustbin. Later on, a builder came round and put boards up at the empty windows and within three days he had put new glass in.

Taken in 2002, showing the former "Lord Nelson", from where the roof of the "Back-house" was blown all across the road and landed on the garage forecourt. [Author]

Maurie at the pub was likewise spurred into action. "I rang the brewery and within less than an hour — about half an hour — I got Marshes, the builders, who used to do a lot of repairs for Strong's (the Romsey brewers who owned the pub). They boarded up all the windows." The army appeared and began clearing up the mess inside the building. "They started up in the attics and picked up the ceiling which had been an old one made up of rushes, wooden slates and plaster. Most of it had come down," and there was white plaster everywhere. The men "came down through the house and right down to the outside and brushed up all the glass."

The blast had blown away the skylight from out-the-back. It had travelled right over the pub roof and landed on the forecourt of Ford's garage, right up against the bridge. "Funny about the skylight!" recalled Inie, "I was upset about it and it was raining."

One of the soldiers, Baydon, a marine, asked her, "Got an umbrella, ma'am?

"Course I've got an umbrella," she replied.

"Well," the young soldier answered, "Push the umbrella up through (the hole left by the vanished window). I'll hold your legs. Push it up through, and then open it out, and then we'll tie it down."

It did the trick. "That umbrella stayed up there a long time!" keeping the rain out.

However, Maurie was very doubtful whether they would be able to open that evening.

"What can we do? We can't open tonight." He moaned.

"Yes, we can!" answered his wife and they did. "Business as usual!" became theirs and the town's slogan, just as it was all over the country at this time.

While the army were busy clearing up the *Lord Nelson*, Marjorie had arrived back in Wareham, worried. She had, of course, heard the sirens go off and most of her fellow workers had gone off into the shelters at the factory. "I knew something had happened, so I kept looking for the thatched roof" of the *King's Arms* as she hurried across the causeway and up St. Martin's Hill, hoping to see the roof still intact. As she climbed the hill, there was the thatch! "It was still there!"

"When I got indoors, I can remember my father came in. It was the only time he put his arms around my mother and gave her a big hug." He was so relieved to have found her alive and unharmed.

By the time Phyl reached the Causeway and the North Bridge there was chaos everywhere – glass, tiles, bricks, all over the place. She began to speculate about where she would have been if she had set off to arrive at the WVS for two o'clock, and felt she might have been in the thick of it.

Ken Ford was now back in the town. He had been over to Bournemouth on his motorbike that morning. "The town was in chaos, glass all over the place!"

Fortunately for Wareham, that was the only serious raid the town had. Minimal by standards elsewhere; nevertheless, because it was so rare, this event has stuck firmly in the minds of all who witnessed it.

Another occasion when the townsfolk were terrified and thought that the end had come was when Arne was bombed in mistake for Holton Heath. On the night of 3rd June 1942, in order to protect the cordite factory, the decoy at Arne was lit and the enemy planes were lured away and pounded Arne, thinking they were devastating the factory. If they had really done this then the British war effort would have been severely hit.

Beryl Binding gave her account of what happened. "You could hear the bombs whistling down. We all dived under the table, with our legs out! What good would it have done. My sister said 'I want a drink of water!' Everytime someone went out to get a glass of water, the bombs'd come down again. We really thought Wareham had been flattened. Then the chap next door to us said 'Can my mother come in with you? She's on her own.' He was a warden.

'What's it like?' we asked.

'It's pretty bad. I don't know what's happening anywhere.'

We had her in. She wouldn't come under the table. She just sat in the chair.

My father was down in Somerset. One of his parents was not well. He rang up a shop in Wareham to see if we were alright. He thought Wareham had been flattened."

On the other hand, there were some who were brave enough to venture out of doors and gaze in wonder, fear and apprehension, at the destruction of Arne.

The full story of this event has been fully dealt with in *Arne. A Purbeck Parish In Peace And War.*

Other raids that are remembered were very minor incidents, like the big raid on Battle of Britain Sunday. F. George, the soldier from Cornwall who was stationed at Northport for a short while, recalled. "It was a busy time and several planes crashed. Some survivors."

Harold Rawles talks about one night when the Germans dropped a lot of incendiaries on the Common. His family had a shelter in their garden, but on this night when the siren went "we heard the crackling and we went up on the Walls, and they dropped all the incendiaries on the Common. You could see them all on the Common glowing."

It may have been this night, or it may have been a totally different one, that Ken Ford recalled an incendiary bomb dropping on Bagg's Mill, but Fred Simpson who worked there managed to defuse it. Later types were less easy to deal with and "exploded as you went to put them out or throw sand over them. They would explode like hell." One of this type fell through the roof of the school in West Street and it sparked away until it was put out by the Fire Brigade.

John Peers in his book recorded two incidents around the station; one when an enemy plane knocked out the overhead telephone cables which ran the link from the telephone exchange to the gunsites at Northport and Arne. The other incident was when a lone aircraft chased a train that had just left the station bound for Wool, and pursued it for several miles.

The river near the old gassworks at North Bridge. Here was where one of the bombs fell during the raid of 16th December 1942. [Author's collection]

Section 3 The Yanks Are Here!

Chapter 8

Their Impact.

For many locals the GIs were indeed "over paid, over sexed and over here," yet at the same time they were, in William Shaw's words, "essentially lonely, horny, transient and, possibly, doomed."

It is impossible for us today to understand just how the Americans felt when they first came to the Isle of Purbeck. Those lads, who came in the first invasion, had been through hell in the fighting in North Africa and in Sicily. Just to get to the peace and quiet of the Dorset countryside seemed heaven and, not having had the pleasure of female companionship since they left America, it is understandable that some were swept off their feet by some of the very friendly Dorset girls, dying for male company at a time when most men over the age of eighteen were away in the British army!

How wonderful must it have seemed to these soldiers to find they were being shipped to England out of the war, at least for the next few months. John Eustace, of the 1st Division, 26th Infantry regiment, B Company, summed up their feelings when he wrote, "Swanage was like heaven after being in North Africa and Sicily." This could apply to any of the local places the Americans were sent to.

Just to reinforce his point, John described how in the Sicily campaign, "we were in a fire fight with the Germans at a place called Barrafranka. During the attack, we lay under a terrific barrage of the Germans. In fact, the barrage was so heavy that we were driven out of our positions… The CO yelled 'Every man for himself!' I am sure we all broke the mile run record that day! Three or four of us found a cave about half to three quarters of a mile from the barrage area. We took refuge in the cave and were surprised to find the cave occupied with Sicilian civilians taking cover from the fighting. The cave was dark, and we thought at first we might have run into Germans, and the civilians thought the same about us! When they found out we were Americans they couldn't do enough for us with wine, bread and cheese."

It is not, therefore, surprising that a sojourn in Britain was such a relief! Some arrived in Liverpool on November 8th. Then they were put on board slow trains with their windows blacked out, bound for Blandford, which they reached the

Bill Lee, at the Hotel Victoria, Swanage, 1944
[Marjorie Jeffries]

following day. Here the vast numbers were divided up. Some stayed, like Angelo Fasano who later remembered building bunk-beds here before moving on to Swanage. Others went to near-by Sturminster Newton. The 16th Division was sent on to Weymouth.

Two days earlier, 26th Division, with John and his fellow soldiers, including Bill Lee, Frank Shaw and Bill Costello had arrived at Wareham. Their division had been sent to Glasgow, from where they too travelled down by train. From Wareham some, like Bill and his mates had to walk to Swanage. "Sunday, a stunning array of military formation as my battalion swung off in cadence, about a thousand strong, strung out, company after company, marching at 'route step', with all the gear infantry use. Luckily, the truck would shuttle back and forth, picking up various units en route, so I don't believe we marched all the way to Swanage." (Bill).

In Swanage, E Company was billeted in the *Grand Hotel*. Though he was not present, William Shaw, in his biography of his uncle Frank's experiences, probably summed it up very aptly when he wrote;-"For men who had been sleeping in cold, muddy foxholes, on stones, or in thin shabby tents for more than a year, the simple comforts of the *Grand Hotel* were lavish beyond expectation. For men who had been washing and shaving out of their helmets, and urinating and emptying their bowels in fields, forests, holes and pits, in cold, rain, snow, heat, day and night – bathrooms with wash basins, tubs, showers and sometimes even hot water awaiting them, were all luxuries." Such words probably hold good for where ever the soldiers found themselves. Others probably found the *Victoria Hotel* just as heavenly.

And not just in Swanage. Carl Best and many others stayed at Wareham. Most of them were in two huts that were built on what had been Churchill's market garden where he grew for his shop in South Street. These were probably not as luxurious as the *Grand* in Swanage, but they had comforts that these battle scarred men found pleasing. The huts were right next to the Church School. For their meals, they went over to the Congregational Chapel. Others were billetted around the town. The Manse in North Street was taken over, so too, was the house on the corner of East Street and Moreton's Lane.

Wherever they went to seemed a luxury for men who had hardly expected to leave Sicily alive. Of the original nearly 15,000 men who had boarded the *Queen Mary* in New York more than a year before, almost 500 had been left behind dead on the battlefields of North Africa and Sicily, a sobering thought that some of those who now found themselves in an earthly paradise tried to suppress.

True, their holiday was regularly punctuated with training – pre-breakfast runs, physical exercises, rifle practice, endless marches, foxhole digging where each soldier had to stay huddled while a tank rolled over it. Many of the troops "pissed and moaned endlessly" (William Shaw), believing that they had earned a good rest. All they wanted was beer, cigarettes, women and sleep, but in no particular order.

"The pubs, that is one of the first places a soldier heads for when they get to a town," confessed Carl Best, one of those GIs. These became their nightly visits at the end of a long day's training; a bath, and good meal, and then a walk or a bus ride down to the local. In Swanage this was the *White Swan*, "a white-washed, shingle-roofed stone structure. It was a traditional pub with low heavy, dark-beamed ceilings, a pleasant variety of local ales and lagers, carpeted floors, small seats, small wooden round tables, and straight, wooden-backed booths. But, most important of all… it had a fireplace and warmth that took the chill out of the damp, tired bones." It is a description that could fit any number of English pubs at that time, including the *King's Arms* at Wareham, which was also popular with the transatlantic visitors.

It was certainly a time when these GIs could relax and enjoy all the comforts that were offered to them, which, they all knew perfectly well, could not last and sooner or later they would be back in the thick of the war, fighting for their lives. But for the moment, that was a thought they refused to consider.

Some things the newcomers found strange about their new environment. English beer was a novelty that took some time to get accustomed to. It was too warm, but they had to get used to it. There was little else to be drunk as the alternative, Scotch, was impossible to get, so warm beer it had to be. As a result in the cozy snug atmosphere of the local pub they came to learn some thing of the area's history, of King Alfred and the Danes, of Oliver Cromwell and his attack on Corfe Castle, and of Hitler's Luftwaffe.

Dart boards were another novelty. It was at *The King's Arms* in Wareham that Carl Best learnt to play this completely new pastime. Cribbage and a card game called Don were also not known across the Atlantic, so when the Americans found Bert Axon playing them on a Sunday lunchtime in the pub they wanted to learn, and he enjoyed teaching them.

Al Crane, sleeping in the back yard of the Kings Arms, 1943/4. Al was killed in action. [Marjorie Jeffries]

New friends could be made while drinking. Thus, it was at the *King's Arms* in Wareham that Marjorie Brewer, the landlord's daughter, met many of the soldiers, who came in to pass the time away. Al Crane, who loved to smoke cigars, came in many times.

However, not all the GIs made a beeline for the local pubs, Angelo and his buddy were not drinkers or smokers, so they avoided them. The only time they went was in Bristol, when they had a three-day pass. Here they started talking to an elderly lady who took them to the Greyhound Races, where under her guidance they backed a winner!

Another thing about this country that Bill Costello still remembers is the fish and chip shops, where he and his pals "enjoyed the fish and chips wrapped in newspaper!" A wonderful new experience! Angelo Fascino is another whose memory of his time in Swanage is of the fish and chips. "They have never been duplicated here in America," he wrote. So much demand was there that the shop in South Street, Wareham, never closed. They used to get their oil from the Americans, who would only use their oil once. According to Bob Thompson, once it had been used, "they'd put it back in the can and take it round to the shop."

Older Wareham folk still talk about the Yanks' tremendous generosity; for example, they were always ready to spread happiness by giving parties. They threw a 21st birthday party for Marjorie Brewer. It was done on a big scale. There was no chance that her parents would have been able to put on more than a small party, not with rationing, but Marjorie was very friendly at this time with a Warrant Officer, Richard Miden. He told her mother quietly; "Don't worry, ma'm, I'll see to it that she has a party."

American Warrant Officers were always referred to as "Mister." Richard was always Mr. Miden. He came from Hastings on the Hudson River in Connecticut. Marjorie thought perhaps he had a garage before he enlisted. He and Marjorie never became engaged, as she already had a regular boyfriend, Howard, who had been a boarder at the pub. He had been a trainee quantity surveyor before he was called up. He went into the RAF and was sent over to Texas to train Americans.

Now in Wareham, Richard came into the pub quite frequently and Marjorie's mum and dad quickly took to him. He became almost one of the family, an acquaintance for Marjorie rather than a boyfriend, but when her twenty-first birthday loomed, he saw to it that she had one that she would never forget.

He had Gene, the army cook, working all the day of her birthday. Marjorie explained, "I went down to the cook-house, which was the old Congregational Schoolroom. I went down there and …well… pies, icecreams; you name it, we had it! I had a wonderful supper. I shall always remember it!" It was on a scale that the locals had not seen since before the war. It was typical of the warm-hearted, generous nature of those boys, Marjorie feels. Later on after the feast, they went on to the Town Hall for a dance.

June Thompson was another who was overwhelmed by their generosity. Gene, the cook, became her boyfriend. He rang up one day to say he had baked her a birthday cake. She called to her brother, Bob, "Can you go and fetch it?" Bob tore over on his bike. When he arrived at the cook-house, Gene said it was not quite done. "He was actually putting the top on. It wasn't a cake but an apple pie, thick, and full of apples. They used to put cinnamon on top."

Kindness like this is still remembered today. "The Americans were so kind." (Bob). In where they had their store cupboard, in the Methodist Schoolroom in Bonnet's Lane, "they had boxes of currants, sultanas and dried stuff." Bob recalled that in the mornings when the children were going to school the soldiers would invite them in. "They could get a handful each. There were some little ones who couldn't reach in, so they built a step up."

They also had a store down where Purbeck View Caravan site now is. It was their dump, and Harold Rawles and his friends spent many a happy hour down there scrounging chewing gum and wooden boxes, which they made great use of.

American trucks were often seen on

The chapel in Church Street which became the Yanks' mess and kitchen [Author's collection]

121

the Sawpits delivering supplies. "If they had a tin of peaches or pears with a dent in it, they'd give it to someone; wouldn't entertain it if it had a dent. Kids would always be down there. They gave away sweets and gum," commented Ray. "We lived like lords!"

Ron Axon was at that time thirteen years old and he and his pals soon made friends with the soldiers. That was not difficult. His garden backed onto where the two huts used by the Americans stood, and the soldiers could offer luxuries undreamed of in wartime Britain. "The yanks had showers! And scented soap! And talcum powder!" instead of the carbolic soap and cold water that Jim and his friends were used to, unless they boiled water in a kettle. "The Gang House Kids!" was what the boys were called by the Americans. "We used to go in and sit on the bed, and they gave us gum, a real luxury."

Captain Kendall was another Yank that Ron still remembers; "a genuine and fair person." He invited the lads to join in playing baseball on the tennis courts in Moreton's Lane, where the old people's home is now. "One day I was hit between the eyes with ball and had two lovely black eyes; messing about; laying on the ground to catch the ball. A yank hit the ball and I lay on the ground; was going to catch it, but it cut straight between the eyes! Worried them to death!"

A friend has since told Marjorie of his vivid memories of the Americans. At the time he was a six year old and lived at Sandbanks. The soldiers used to come down there to the beach for training. "I had my first orange and my first banana. I had never seen them before!"

Bob Thompson was a typical teenager at the time, always hungry. On one occasion, when he went over to their cook house, a soldier came in for his breakfast.

"What do you want? Pork chops?" he was asked.

"Yea!" came the reply.

Bob's eyes opened wide, as "out came a box about 2 feet by 1 foot, and 4 inches deep. He (Gene) opened it, and there were all these pork sausages inside! He put oil into the frying pan," whereas Bob was only used to lard. The cook pulled out two sausages and put them in, and turned round to Bob and his friend.

"Would you like a chop?" he asked.

"We said, 'Yes, please!'

Two more went in for us, out came a loaf and he sliced it. Out came a pack of butter, a 4 lb piece. I'd never seen so much butter in one lump! They said 'Help yourself!' We got a knife and I sliced this butter off nearly as thick as the bread and laid it on. Then when Gene had cooked it, he laid the boiling hot chop on the bread. It went zizz! And melted the butter. Another piece on top, and we munched it. It ran down my face! I can taste it now! It was like Christmas and birthdays and everything all wrapped up together!"

Other Wareham schoolboys were drawn to that kitchen. "When we came out of school, we used to go down the Congregational Chapel and have tea. We had food that we normally wouldn't have seen - for example, Corn fritters, peaches – marvellous things."

"They were very generous to us kids," said David Grant, "and gave us sweets and chocolate. They used to dish out sweets like polo mints!" Such luxuries Bob Thompson also remembered "We used to sit back on a table (during filmshows put on by the Yanks) with a galvanised bucket between us, Vic and me, of canned fruit that the men had had at lunchtime, and we used to help ourselves! That's where I got my love of pineapples! They were so lovely!"

Rear: Big Mac (just in view), Tommy Bergin, Joe Rudd, Joe Costello (from Ohio) Front left: Al Crane, ?, ? 1st Division, 26th Infantry, outside "Kings Arms" 1943/ 4 [Marjorie Jeffries]

Ray Watkins remembered the Christmas they were here, Christmas 1943, when "the top brass came down from Binnegar Hall, which was their Headquarters, to Bennetts' shop in East Street. They asked Mr. Farrell, who owned the business then, if they could cook their turkeys in the ovens.

Mr. Farrell said; 'Yes. You can, but not when we're baking bread!'

'Oh! Sure! We can come when you ain't cooking bread! When will that be?'

'In the afternoons.'

'That's fine! That's what we want!"

When they did turn up, they came with huge trays of turkeys, and other trays with joints of meat on, large pieces of beef, lamb and pork, that when cooked required carving up. "The big trays we used to put our bread on, they filled with pastry and put mincemeat on top." In addition, the soldiers made their own bread rolls. Observing all of this, as he came into the bakehouse while serving in the shop, Ray commented;- 'They're going to do very well for Christmas!" But he realised that the meat was for those who were doing the hard work in the bakehouse. Every so often, they would take a fresh roll, slice it open and fill it with the cooked meat.

And Ray was not forgotten. "Every time I went into the bakehouse, they'd say, 'Do you wanta roll, kid?' You could choose what meat you wanted in it. I stuffed myself that afternoon, in between trying to serve someone in the shop. That was a momentous occasion, that was!" A memory that has stayed with Ray ever since.

John Symonds also recalled the wonderful parties the Americans threw for the children. He was about five or six at the time and very impressed.

It may have been at one of these that one American captain was so taken with Herbie Elmes' conjuring tricks that after this, every time he saw Herbie, he would buy him a whisky; presumably that is, if it was obtainable!

It was their wonderful apples pies and meringues that June Thompson recalled. They would take out two or three pies" to Sandford Hotel where the Rowleys did meals.

Boys were fascinated by the American motors, which they saw all over the town. "They used to leave their jeeps unattended," said Harry Rawles, recalling the thrill of climbing aboard and putting feet on the pedals and moving along the road. No wonder he commented; "Great excitement for us youngsters!"

Once Bob felt he had just missed the thrill of a lifetime. It was when he went into the kitchen one day and found Gene was talking with another sergeant. They were obviously discussing a visitor to the kitchen.

The sergeant asked, "Did He come?"

"Yes," said Gene, "He came!"

"About what time?"

"About two o'clock! ... after everybody else had gone. He's in an exhibition at Weymouth tonight."

Bob continued "I thought a bit, and then asked 'Who are you talking about?'

'Joe Louis!'

'Joe Louis! One of the biggest names in boxing at that time, and, I could have sat next to him and touched him!"

Other memories people still have are of the Yanks' tremendous enthusiasm. Their jeeps were robust vehicles, and some of the soldiers used to try and get them over the steep hills in the Purbecks, trying to get as high as they could. "I never saw one come to grief." commented David. Bill Lee was one of those GIs who tried this dare-devil exploit, driving his jeep up the very steep slopes of Corfe Castle.

One Yank that Ron Axon got on well with was George Peloso whose job it was to look after the army boilers for the huts. "Ever so nice chap he was," recalled Ron, "but one night he had a drink too many and got himself locked out! So, he got an axe and smashed the door down!" Ron regrets he does not know what happened to George for this.

In fact, Ron and his pals got on well with many of the soldiers. "They had time for us local lads," he now observes. His garden backed on to where they were billeted and he begged his mother to do the laundry of one of his new friends, Frankie Boteler, though everyone called him Manny. "I would collect it. My mother would wash, iron and return it. I carried it back." Another soldier "always came over from Swanage to get his laundry done. He'd park his jeep outside, and he would come on indoors and sit down. Mother didn't like that! She was old-fashioned. She used to like the chap but not his manner. Other mums did the washing for other soldiers. They all used to compare their shirts; how they were ironed; how their uniforms were pressed, and all that; they'd take bets on it!" Ron reckoned that they told him that his mother's work always came out on top!

With local girls pining for male company and many Americans determined to get the most out of few months of rest before the horrors of war that they would surely be pitched back into sooner or later, it was natural that many of the local girls had a wonderful time.

One of them was June Thompson. "The girls (in the accounts department where she worked) were very nice, but I hadn't really made any friends," she now recalls. "Then, in December, one of the girls – we were in the Ladies' – said, 'I don't suppose you'd like to come out tonight or tomorrow?'

"What for?" I said.

'You know the American soldiers have come to Wareham.' Since I was so new to the area, I'd been here for just over a month, I didn't know. 'It would make up a six.'

'With whom?'

So she explained that she and her friend had American boyfriends, and that there was another American who would like to meet an English girl.'

'I don't know what my parents would say!'

'Well, you're more than welcome! I think he's a very nice boy.'

My father was the man of the house, so I decided to try to coax mother first.

'What will you do?' she asked.

'Don't know. Pictures or something. It would be nice to meet one or two people.'

'It won't be anything of this serious rubbish, would it?'

'Of course not! It's just one evening, that's all."

With that her mother suggested she ask her father. "My father being a man of the world said, ' I don't see why not."

Thus it was that June met the two girls and the three soldiers at Wareham Cross. "I can remember the dress I wore –woollen—December time — it was cold – afternoon frock. I thought 'I don't know what my father would say.'

It was lovely there – a beautiful log fire – a real pub lounge. I was introduced to the three boys. I was quite amazed. They all spoke differently, with different accents! I thought, 'this isn't like the pictures, like Hollywood! — because that's all you knew about Americans was the films, so I thought 'Isn't it strange?"

The boy she was introduced to was a quiet spoken lad with a soft drawl, sounding completely different to the other two. "As we talked, the evening wore on and it looked as though we weren't going anywhere else. The boy I was introduced to, Gene, Eugene, suggested we went and sat by the fire, so we left the other four and went and sat by the fire and just talked. We never stopped talking. We hit it off from that moment on. I asked my parents if I could bring him home for Christmas, and they said 'Yes!'"

This romance blossomed. Gene was invited over to meet her parents. He was the cooks' sergeant and worked in what had been the Congregational Church Schoolroom in Lady St. Mary's Lane.

Private Joe Catt was billeted here in this old house, with a farm next to it. The farm had two land girls on it, one of them, Jess Holford's daughter, married a Mr Wenby from Dorchester. Joe is uncertain now where this house was. [Joe Catt]

The first time he came he had been up practically all the previous night working in the kitchens. "I introduced him to my parents and family, and in the middle of the afternoon I suddenly realised the boy I fancied was not there anymore. He was in the sitting room under a blanket asleep. Mother had put him on the settee, lit the fire, and he slept the whole afternoon away. He was quickly accepted into my family."

Joe Catt (left) and another sergeant in their camp, somewhere east of Dorchester, 1943. Joe is now uncertain whether it was near Wareham. [Joe Catt]

The romance went well. On Sundays she took him to church at Lady St. Mary's, and then they would go to his canteen and have lunch with eighty odd troops. June still remembers the taste of those southern fried chicken Sunday dinners. Dried carrots with sultanas was another thing that was new to June. "I thought it quite delicious." Food was plentiful here, at a time when food was rationed.

On Saturdays they went to the cinema, booking in advance one of the "lovers' seats" at the back, two seats together without a separating armrest. Going to the pictures was the obvious thing to do of an evening. The cinema was at the height of its popularity even before the Yanks arrived, with long queues stretching far down West Street on a Friday or Saturday evening. With the arrival of the Yanks the queues became even longer and more frequent.

Occasionally, when something went wrong and the film broke down, "there'd be catcalls. There were usually one or two Americans there who had had experience of projectors back home, and they would be able to go and sort it out."

And what went on in back rows of cinemas all over the country where there were GIs became legendary! Though this was probably no different to what went on before the Yanks arrived or what went on after the war ended.

The GIs also put on films in their cook-house in the Congregational Chapel on a Sunday evening. "These were tremendous occasions," recalled David Grant. Here, he had a chance of seeing many films before they went on general release, like *Higher And Higher*, with Frank Sinatra, which even now sticks in his memory. During these evenings several local girls also had a whale of a time but for completely different reasons.

June and Gene's friendship grew more serious. "He went into my father's office in March and asked 'Could we become engaged?'" June did not know of this visit until one evening when he came over and all her sisters, mum and dad were there and he presented her with an engagement ring.

Dances and socials were common where the soldiers dance bands played. In Swanage's Church Hall it was the First Division who played, and that's where the tunes of Glenn Miller were first heard; *In The Mood, American Patrol,* as well as the others that were known, like Cole Porter's *Begin The Beguine.* Their great playing and the marvellous tunes are what Marjorie remembers. "They had some terrific dance bands." Consequently, these evenings at the Wareham's Town Hall were extremely popular, not just because the lads were expert players, but it was where a young lady could go, find company and enjoy herself, Moreover, she could learn the intricate, but exhilarating steps of the new dance that the Yanks had brought with them –the jitterbug. "We thought it was marvellous!"

But, for Marjorie, it was New Year's Eve, 1943, that stays forever in her mind. The Yanks "thought it was marvellous. They'd never seen anything like it before." Perhaps it was the setting, dancing round Wareham Cross out in the street. Perhaps it was the warm acceptance of the soldiers by the townsfolk as members of the family. Perhaps it was the sure knowledge that such happiness could not last, and that 1944 would bring blood, agony, and death. But on this wonderful evening, everyone could forget all this and just wallow in the magic of the night and the music. And what music! All those Glenn Miller arrangements! Whenever Marjorie hears his *Moonlight Serenade,* back come the memories! She was deliriously happy.

Some GIs, however, were not satisfied with such innocent pleasures and wanted to go further, and what went on under Wareham Bridge was nobody's business! With little female company since they had left the States, all some of the lads wanted was sex, and some local girls and women, as elsewhere, enjoyed surrendering,

Marjorie Brewer and Richard Miden at the back of "Kings Arms". Behind the tree are the horse stables. [Marjorie Jeffries]

where ever there were any horny, handsome, lonesome soldiers. They argued, no doubt, that they were only doing their bit to keep up the morale of these lonely boys.

Another who was keen to do her best for the soldiers was one of the two women in the signal box at Corfe Castle. They were employed to work the box after the men had been called up. One came from Swanage, her colleague came from Wareham. Both had to cycle each day. Sometimes they did not turn up and the stationmaster had to go and hope to get one of the retired signalmen who lived in the square at Corfe to come. It was vital to have staff on duty at Corfe because the line was a single track and safety regulations decreed that the tablet for the next part of the line from Corfe had to be given to the train driver. When the Swanage woman knew that a train had American soldiers on board, she would get David Grant to do her duty in the box. In return, David was given a lot of chewing gum.

One Wareham woman was well known for entertaining GIs. Once when her old man came home on Embarkation Leave, they couldn't find her anywhere. The assumption was that she was with her "Darling Elmer."

David Grant recalled that the walls of the town were at this time protected by barbed wire, but what has stuck in his memory was the sight of the wire being covered in condoms! The Americans were issued with these in shoe boxes. The Canadians and the British were not.

Beryl recalled that at parties the Yanks always used to give children balloons, or, at least, she says they were called balloons. In later years, she is not sure that these long transparent things really were balloons.

While the sexual exploits of some American soldiers coloured the views of most English people, who tended to regard all Yanks as "over-sexed," many soldiers did not want to go further than just companionship, if indeed that far. Angelo and his buddy had no wish to be untrue to their respective fiancees back home, so for them dating was out.

The relationship with local people was two way. The American boys did bring happiness, generosity and high-spirits, but they gained in return in the invitations into local homes, being treated as members of the family.

Fresh vegetables straight from the allotment were other great luxuries. Bill Lee's memory goes back to these wonderfully homely meals, delicious especially when washed down with glasses of beer. He and his pals were, and still are, eternally grateful for all these local people who gave them friendship and warmth.

One thing that did impress the locals was that the majority of the Americans did not swear. June can testify to this, in that her boyfriend, Gene, never said a word out of place. The only time he was crude stands out clearly in her mind. They were just coming out of the chapel and were walking past one of the houses on the left when from the window came the voice of one well-known girl who certainly had a reputation for keeping company with a lot of Yanks; "Hello, Gene!"

Being polite, he replied, "Hello!"

"We walked on," recalled June, "and he looked at me, and I looked at him. He said, ' She'll do anything with a cock except eat it!"

Friendship was given in other ways, too. Christmas Eve 1943 was very cold. The band were playing carols in the Town Hall and Percy Best met one of the American sergeants whom he invited back for coffee and later to stay the night and spend the festive day with them.

Percy was also a help to Eddie Schwarz, on another occasion. Eddie was a Lt. Corporal and had been driving a tank when he knocked a woman down on the Dorchester/Bridport road. He was naturally very alarmed about what might happen to him. When he told Percy all about it Percy rang Dorchester Hospital, who told him that the woman had been discharged. Therefore, he was able to reassure the frightened lad that no further action would be taken by the police. At this, Eddie began to cheer up. Percy took him home, and after that, the Bests' house in Bell's Orchard Lane became something of second home to him.

In various ways, local people took these transatlantic boys to their hearts and often made them part of their family. Yet, there were things about them that surprised Wareham folk. For example, compared with their British buddies, they were very casual. Marjorie Brewer remembered looking through the windows of her pub at one of the many Yankie columns marching through the town. There they were sauntering along the street in the gutter and smoking cigarettes and looking "a right shower! British soldiers were never allowed to do that. They always had to march smartly."

Another thing that puzzled was the Yanks' treatment of their coloured colleagues. It

Eddie Schwartz is in the centre of this group in front of cottages in East Street. Photo sent to Percy Best [Author's collection]

was the first time that most English people had seen a coloured man, apart from on the silver screen, but locals accepted them readily as being part of the US Army. This many Yanks found perplexing. Their attitude was different. The coloured soldiers' freedom to leave their billets was highly restricted. Some were up at Binnegar Hall, while others were "stationed around Organford but, wherever they were, they were only let out on certain days. They didn't have the freedom the white ones did," (Bob) and many English people were frankly quite shocked by this discrepancy. June's father once asked Gene, who came from the South, why they treated their coloured soldiers differently.

"You've got to live with them," came the answer.

It was the same answer that June said she got in the 1990s when she asked the same question on a visit to the USA, but this attitude certain surprised English people during the war.

Not all locals, however, were over-keen on the visitors. Some girls found their attentions alarming. One who did was Phyl Marsh, who had been evacuated from Arne after the big raid there in June 1942, when the village was pounded with bombs. The Germans thought they had found Holton Heath, which they were determined to destroy. This trick of using Arne as a decoy worked, but the villagers lost their homes and had to move out. Phyl and her invalid mother were lucky in finding a house in Sandford Road. Phyl joined the WVS.

One evening a crowd of Yanks visited the canteen which the WVS ran on the Quay, and Phyl was a little apprehensive about what might happen when they shut up the canteen at 10 o'clock. She would have to walk up through the middle of the town, out to the station and up the Sandford Road. She was well aware that it would be very dark. There were no streets lights on, so she would be alone. Though she had done the route many times, she confessed that "it was always eerie!" Besides, tonight she was bothered about some Yanks following her. Fortunately, she persuaded a colleague to walk part of the way with her, but the women were aware as they went on that they were being followed by two tall men. At St. Martin's Church, her friend said she would have to leave her. She lived down East Street. She did not want to go back down the main street and have to pass the soldiers, so she cut across by the church and went home that way.

Bucking up courage, Phyl continued down past the *Lord Nelson* and across the Causeway, still being followed. Perhaps she was now dreading the walk up Sandford Road, where there would be no passers-by. She was relieved to see a Wareham train had pulled into the station and lots of people were coming out, including some English lads. "I knew one by name through being in the canteen. I'd never really spoken to him before, and I called him by name. He said;-

'What's the matter?'

I said, 'I've got these two Yanks following me.'

He told me not to be afraid, as some of our boys would probably be just as bad. I looked round, and the two Yanks had gone back up Shatter's Hill."

On another occasion, when she came off duty and had walked as far as the *Lord Nelson,* a jeep pulled up in front of her, and the driver asked to take her home. Whether he was genuinely concerned or just wanted a good time, she did not debate, but refused his offer, protesting that she had only a few yards to walk. Eventually, he got tired of inviting her and drove off. Phyl was very relieved.

On another evening, she was rescued by her neighbour, Mr. Brown, who saw her being followed and shouted. At that, her pursuers gave up, and her friend accompanied her all the way home.

Some men were even less keen on the newcomers, blaming them for the shortage of drink in the pubs. The usual Yankee response was "We're fighting for you!"

To which locals would reply, "Ah! But we'll be here when you've gone!"

Chapter 10

After The Yanks.

This wonderful warmth could not last. After all, the war was still going on, and the Allied military commanders were planning their invasion of the continent. The Yanks knew that sooner or later they would be part of that invasion. In Spring 1944 their 'holiday' came abruptly to an end.

From many places all over England, men and equipment were being gathered on the south coast, so much so that local people knew something was up. One GI commented; "It's a wonder this island doesn't sink, — with the weight of all these tanks and equipment on it!"

In Wareham, just before D-Day, there was a huge gathering of troops on the Recreation Ground. Ray Herridge is convinced Winston Churchill came down and spoke there. "It was solid with troops. Nearest I could get — the Americans were armed with guns — was standing up on the workhouse wall. There was this American somebody who came — landed in a little aeroplane in what was Galton's Field next to the school. There was a fellow in British uniform and this man in a black coat and hat, right down at the end of the Recreation Ground. You couldn't see very well. The Americans in their great big lorries were all down the Common, and some of them had got stuck in the bog. We had the job afterwards of picking up the paper!"

The Brewers had a cousin in Salisbury, who wanted to come stay about this time, as she had often come in the past, but Wareham was now a restricted area. Marjorie recalled, "My mother went to the police and asked if she could come and stay with us. They said, 'No. This is a top security area. No visitors whatsoever.' So she wasn't allowed to come."

Then came the day when the troops moved out. "The wonderful six months," in Marjorie's words, were over. Lots of people stood on the railway platform to wave goodbye, as the trains pulled out for Weymouth and Bournemouth. It was as if the lights in the town (had there been lights) had gone out. "All gone! Wareham was dead! We girls didn't know what to do with ourselves!" (Marjorie)

Then came the wait for what was surely going to happen … the invasion of France. Of D-Day morning Marjorie's memories are still vivid. "I was on night shift. All night long the planes were going over, row after row after row after row, droning across. We thought that something was up. We knew they were all ours, and they were going across our factory all night. Of course, when we got home we heard that the Second Front had started. I shall never forget that night."

The manoeuvre of men from the First Division of the United States Army from the Purbecks to a cross channel port … many went to Plymouth … and then over to Normandy, is part of international history. The official book on the First Division of the United States Army, *Danger Forward,* gives Portland as the port from which the soldiers crossed the Channel. From all over the south of England other divisions sailed as part of Operation Overlord.

'Omaha' was the beach that was assigned to the First Division. It was the worst of all the beaches, with the result that the fighting was very fierce. Many did not survive. Many of those young men who had enlivened Wareham were among the 2811 officially noted as being killed on 'Omaha.' Another 5,744 were recorded as missing or captured, while 13,546 were described as seriously wounded. "They didn't know what they were going to face," commented Marjorie later.

Gene was not among those on the Normandy beaches. As a cook and not a fighting soldier, he was not needed until the beachhead was well and truly captured. "All the troops took their rations. They couldn't set up kitchens until they were established in France," June explained years later. This meant that he and June could have a few more days together. Their last night was on June 6th, when "they went to Bournemouth. He came over to say 'Goodbye.' He didn't go across until June 13th, I think."

For those of his countrymen who were on the beaches and who managed to endure and get through that day they still had to push back the Germans, and though it may appear today in popular culture that the war was virtually over after D-Day, in reality this was far from the case. Many a grim battle took place on the road to Berlin during those eleven months before Germany finally surrendered.

Thousands of young soldiers never made it to the end. June's Gene did not. He was killed at the village of Caumont, not that many miles inland from the French beaches. He had been over in France only about three weeks. Caumont has been described as "a bold fist of a hill dominating the surrounding county." (Chester Wilmot). Here, Americans met stiff resistance from the Germans and were held up for several days (12th – 14th June). It was here during a heavy barrage that a piece of shrapnel caught Gene and killed him.

During the next three months the Allies slowly pushed the enemy back, with the First Division skirting south round Paris and northwards to the Belgian border. They encountered more fighting outside Mons. Their next objective, Aachen, was an even tougher nut to crack. It was just inside Germany, and to capture it the soldiers had to smash through the strong Seigfried Line, which was being assaulted all along its length.

"Aachen was a coal-producing centre and a key point in the Seigfried Line defences. Aachen was a symbol of heroic resistance for the Germans as Stanlingrad had been for the Russians," says the official history of the First Division. "The German people had been positively assured that Aachen could not be taken."

Chester Wilmot has put the assault on this city in context by referring to what the rest of the American and Allied troops were doing. They were attacking all along the Seigfried Line. The First Division did meet stubborn resistance which took about a week to overcome before the Commandant there surrendered. Perhaps the official history is a little simplistic in it's "Aachan crumbled and Nazi honour received a shattering blow." It was during this operation that Marjorie's friend Richard died.

In their slow advance the Allies captured many prisoners. Most were German, and among them was Butch Jaeger. He was captured by the Americans and sent to a prison camp between Paris and Cherbourg. There, he witnessed the arrival of a train bringing another load of his countrymen. He was horrified to discover the carriages had been so packed that 138 of them were found dead, suffocated, when the train arrived. After the war ended, he heard a rumour that the prisoners were going to be handed over to the French, an idea which no one wanted. When the men were given a chance to volunteer to come to England, Butch took it, and eventually found himself in Wareham.

But that was sometime after the war, in 1947. In 1944 the war was far from over. There was much more confrontation and the German army fought back savagely in Hurtzen Forest, "a forest nobody had paid much attention to before, but will never be forgotten," (*Danger Forward*) because of the numbers killed.

Then, on 20th November 1944, the Germans launched their great counter offensive against the Allies in the Ardennes, which lasted throughout the coldest months of the winter, and did not end until 6th February 1945. Many soldiers were killed during the savage fighting there. Finally, three months later, Germany did surrender, in May 1945.

Marjorie was still at Holton Heath when news came through that the war in Europe was over.

"We jumped for joy!"

Ray Herridge heard the news as he was walking home from a farm at Worgret after delivering milk. A lady ran up to him and kissed him! "Lovely!" he confesses, but then he says he was often being kissed by ladies on his milk-round.

Ray Watkins, the Wareham Bevin boy, was less enthusiastically greeted on the coalfields of Durham. He did not hear about the end of the war until his shift was over and he came up in the cage. Then he heard about the surrender.

It was in Italy, where his regiment were still fighting, that Archie Brennan, the Desert Rat heard the news.

All over the country people went wild that night, and Wareham was no exception. All the pent-up emotions of the last six years suddenly erupted. That evening there was dancing round the Cross. Bob Thompson, then not yet sixteen, recalled recently that the music was provided by records from an army vehicle near the *Red Lion*, with a loud speaker on top, and people dancing around it. Joe Curtis, who kept the *Horse and Groom* on St John's Hill never lost an opportunity to play his accordion. He joined in..

After nearly six years of restrictions everyone went wild. They had not had anything to celebrate for six years, and they were determined to show it. For Bob, it was his first drink!

"Vic and I said 'Let's have beer!'

We decided to go and get it, as we were fifteen or sixteen. There was still 'the Bottle and Jug' at most pubs. We decided to go to the *Duke of Wellington* in East Street. Lots of people there and on the pavement outside. I went in and got two bottles of light ale. That's all I knew as my father was not a drinking man. It was obvious we were under age, but no one cared that night. Anyway, we drank it, and I said, 'Right, Vic, it's your turn!' but he chickened out!"

It was also the night Bob kissed a girl. She worked in the Co-op. "I always fancied her, but I don't think I had actually spoken to her before!" But it was a night to enjoy life.

His sister was thoroughly enjoying herself too. She was among those dancing around the Cross. "A band came in from Bovington, and we danced all night!" reminisced June Thompson. "I walked home and got back about 4.00 in the morning."

Marjorie's memories are of standing outside her pub with another chap there from the *King's Arms* at Stoborough, deliriously happy, when "the daughter of the people there (at Stoborough) came by in a big army lorry. She was hanging out the back and called 'Come on, Min! Come and join us!' And we went round in that lorry!" Other lorries were also going around as well, all filled with girls.

When the euphoria died down there was a need for a more tangible celebration, and all over the country people got together with their neighbours to organise street parties. Once again, Wareham was no exception. "We went mad." (Joan Anderson). Beryl Binding described hers, down the road. "We all dressed up, and all the streets had their own parties. Everyone turned out, and we had a wonderful night. We all clubbed in and made something. Never been another like it since!"

There were street parties everywhere, "practically the whole town being covered," wrote the local reporter. That for Church Street, St. John's Hill, Church Green and the Quay was held on St. John's Hill, with a fancy dress parade, judged by the Mayor and Mayoress, Mr and Mrs J. Norman. Than about sixty children tucked into tea with thirty old folks joining them. Sports and a tug-of-war followed. Herbie Elmes then did his turn. "Each child received a cash gift of 3s 6d (17½p) and a bag of chips," and dancing and music followed well into the evening. A similar treat was held at the Junior School for North Street, St. Martin's Lane and Edward Crescent.

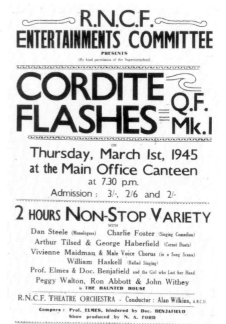

[Hughie Elmes collection]

This (or another party for North Street) was the work of Charlie Bussell, from the sweetshop whose windows had blown out in the raid of 1942. He raised a lot of money for it and organised it.

Some did hold their parties actually in the street. After all, with little traffic around, this was not difficult to do. Those in Mill Lane, however, hired Jeff's Market and had, in Joan's words, "a beautiful party up there. All the old folks came as well."

Herbie Elmes, the local magician and comic, found himself in great demand all over the area often with his side-kick, Ted Benjafield; at Branksome on the Gas Works Ground; at Upton; at the *Junction Hotel* in Hamworthy, to list but a few.

One party that most older people still remember and one whose photograph has been reproduced in many books, was the dinner at the Town Hall on 2nd April 1946 organised by Dulcie Yates. She had been collecting for it for some time beforehand, and "put on a wonderful party" (Marjorie). 150 ex-servicemen and women were there. After a silence in memory of those who did not come back, Dulcie proposed a toast to all ex-servicefolk and to those who were still overseas. During the speeches, the Mayor Cllr and Rev H. Kirkpatrick paid Mrs Yates a tremendous tribute for writing to so many local men and girls during the war. She

Dulcie's Welcome Home party at the Town Hall on 2nd April 1946.

Menu;

Cream of Celery Soup

Cold Meats, Mixed Pickles, Beetroot, Mashed Potato.

Cream Trifle and Ice Cream.

Coffee.

Cigarettes.

Entertainment;

Music by Leonard's Accordian Band
The Human Dynamo .... Elmes & Benjafield
Dance .... Brenda Bailey
Song .... T. Williams
Dance .... Chris Cleall
The Milkman (Sketch) .... Elmes, Benjafield & Boyce
Song .... T. Wellstead
Dance .... Chris & Brenda
Comedy Conjuring .... Elmes & Benjafield
Song .... G. Pitman
Football Pools (Sketch) .... Elmes, Benjafield & Boyce
Entertainer .... A. Boyce
The Bare Truth (Sketch) .... H. Elmes
Community Singing

God Save The King

The
Duke of Wellington
Welcome Home Party

The Corn Exchange.
Wareham

April 2nd,
1946

had written "Heaven knows how many letters!"

A few months later, when Japan surrendered, everyone went wild again. More street parties were organised, and again Herbie Elmes was in demand. His records mention parties in Worgret, Stoborough, Holton Heath, Furzebrook, East Stoke, and Sandford House locally, and further afield in Hamworthy, Parkstone, Upton, Bere Regis and Sturminster Marshall.

At one of these street parties, this incorrigible entertainer introduced *The Tantinoby Trot*, a very impromptu dance routine which he first danced with Freddie Gibson. Thereafter, it was always in demand and was preformed all over the place, at street parties, variety shows; in fact, where ever Herbie appeared. There was no set tune, but if someone provided suitable music then *The Trot* was shown off. The day after it was first performed, Pinkie Skewes, the headmaster of the private school in the town, came up to Herbie and observed, "Do you know, Mr. Elmes, I never knew you were an acrobat. You should be on the stage." Herbie confessed later that he was covered in bruises from having fallen down as part of the dance routine.

Ken Ford, out in the Far East, missed all this jubilation. He was in the jungle of Malaya, and did not hear anything of the German surrender or of Japan's capitulation. He returned to England by ship, which took several months. "A thousand of us on board this ship ... terrifically crowded, especially in the bilges

David Grant in 1947

below deck in the tropics ... climbed over six other people before you got into bed at the top."

David Grant went up to London to see the Victory Parade. He had been given a couple of tickets. "We went to Southall Barracks for a couple of nights. We went down to the Victoria Memorial outside Buckingham Palace," from where they saw the parade. Going back that night to Southam, David was so tired from standing all day, that he fell asleep hanging on to the strap.

More parties, often for just the family and friends, were held when men came back from the war. People who had not been speaking to each other for years now kept asking their neighbours "When's so-and-so coming home?"

Some, of course, did not return. The war memorial records the names of 27 men, far fewer than the numbers killed in the First World War. But for their families, it was much too high a figure, and of course, it does not contain the names of the boys from across the Atlantic who did not survive and who were, temporarily at least, Wareham's.

With peace came new problems, such as what to do with the prisoners of war here. In the last months of the war the army camp near the station was used to accommodate a number of Italian prisoners. They were interned in the army camps at Tantinoby or Furzebrook. When Harold Rawles first started driving, he had to take some of them round to the sawmills. He always remembers seeing one Italian at the mill out at Lulworth, cutting out wooden soles for clogs on a bandsaw, which was very close to his fingers.

Many of the young lads of the town treated them unkindly and jeered at them whenever they saw them. They were easily identified by the dark diamond piece of cloth on the back of their jackets. After Italy gave up, these prisoners were allowed out into the town. "Us, youngster, used to get up by the church (St. Martin's) and throw stones at them. Once or twice, we got them cornered in Trinity Lane, and let them have it. Many were interned in the old army camp near the station. They came up to the big school, the chief one, and the older boys were lined up in the hall. He (the chief one) came on the stage, with Fred Stuckey, the headmaster. He said, 'We are no longer enemies. We are your friends.'

And I tell you what! We threw everything at them — chairs — whatever we could find. It was a riot! They came round with a stick, lashing out at us. He (the chief) ran for it. 'It is the end of the friendship!' It (the riot) gradually died down."

Surprisingly, German prisoners seem to have been treated better. Again, Ray remembers seeing several German pilots who had been captured "sitting in a wagon … youngsters they were … not much older than us, they were …

Butch Jaeger and Joan on their wedding day.
[Butch Jaeger]

covered in wet blankets … it was raining … and the people (who were in charge) were in Burgess's café having a cup of tea."

Later came other German prisoners of war, soldiers who had been taken on the continent. Butch Jaeger described the camp as having two kitchens, one for the Germans and the other for English soldiers. He chose to work in the one for the English as he knew enough English to get by. He and another prisoner ran the kitchen between them.

Butch found the commander there a "nice chap really," whose friends, Mr. and Mrs. Wilson, ran the *Grosvenor Hotel* in Swanage They wanted somebody in the kitchens, Butch explained recently. "He came to me and asked me if I'd go. I said 'I don't mind,' so I went. They (the Wilsons) had been at the Germany Embassy before the war. They could speak German. He was a very nice chap, and we got on like a house on fire." Butch was perhaps lucky to have this break. Perhaps he was the sort of chap that people cannot help liking. Perhaps a bit of both, but he did well, found a lovely girl in spite of her father's initial opposition and was able to make a good life in the area.

For Harold, Vic, Archie, Ken and thousands of others who served in the armed forces, the end of war could bring personal problems. They had to pick up their civilian lives and adjust to peace, as did Bevin Boys, like Ray Watkins. Widows had to struggle on as best they could, though some of them had been doing this for several years. For some that was not easy; for others it was incredibly difficult. To complicate matters, there were the background problems that they could do nothing about, the economy and politics. All this is a tremendously important part of the town's history, just as it is part of the history of the country, but that requires another book.

Those Americans who had been very much part of the town for about seven months and who did survive went back home, a few with Wareham girls. Shirley Ash, Maurie's daughter, of the *Lord Nelson*, was of them. But many of the Yanks never forgot England. They continued to write, as many still do, to the people who had befriended them. As one of these, Bill Costello, wrote in 1995, "we made a lot of friends, some of whom still last today." For Carl Best, "The town of Wareham was a wonderful place. We could not have been treated nicer or better had we been at our own homes. The people were just wonderful. As for what the people gave us; some gave as a parent would – their love for a child, which is what a lot of us were – just overgrown children."

Appendix
Soldiers Killed in World War II.

Based on notes compiled by Percy Best.

L.A.C. Edmund Arnold,

Signaller M. Arnold. .... two brothers, sons of Mr. and Mrs. F. Arnold of West Walls. Their father was a blacksmith for Newbery's.

FT. Sgt. E. Bartlett.

Gunner W. Biles.

L/B G. Brown .... killed in the Western Desert; lived in Mill Lane, brother of E. Brown, who later became Mayor of Wareham.

Pt. William G. Burden .... was the first Wareham soldier to be killed in the Western Desert, in December 1942, just after his 30th birthday; lived in Nundico and worked for Whittles, the butchers; known to everyone as 'Bimbo'; a good snooker, billiards, tennis and cricket player.

Petty Off. Alan Carick .... son of Southern Electric Board Manager.

L/S Stephen Comden.

Sig. Leon Day .... son of Mr. and Mrs. Day of Mill Lane.

Seaman R. Diment.

Pt. J. Donaghue.

Seaman Frank Herd.

Pt. A. Howarth.

Seaman L. Lawrence.

Pt. Sid Marshallsay.

Stoker Harold Morgan .... killed abroad *H.M.S. Victory*, 1942, but interred in Wareham cemetery.

Sgt. Peter Nichol.

Seaman Albert Orchard.

Pt. Charles Samways.

John William Savage .... killed when *The Royal Oak* was hit in Scarpa Flow and keeled over, (details from J. Murphy, *Dorset At War*, p.3.)

A.B. Wilfrey Selby .... related to the two Selbys killed in WW1.

Pt. Raymond Singer.

Sgt. Dennis Slade .... lived in Roper's Lane. Percy last saw him on Christmas Day, when they were singing *Once In Royal David's City*. He was reported as missing on his next mission.

L/Corp. Horace Slade .... No relation to Dennis; known as 'Nunc'.

St. Dennis Snell .... son of Dr. Snell of The Manor House. Killed in D- Day, Percy thought.

Sapper S. Spreadbury .... His father was one of Wareham's policemen.

LT. Sgt. William Thomas.

Pt. A. William Velnick .... His father and mother were the Master and Matron of the Wareham Workhouse.

Index

Source List.

Bibliography.

M.R.Bowditch, *Cordite-Poole,* not dated.

M. R. Bowditch & L. Hayward, *Royal Naval Cordite Factory; Holton Heath,* Wareham, 1996.

Terence Davis, *Arne; A Purbeck Parish in Peace & War,* Wincanton, 2000.

Terence Davis, *Wareham, Gateway To Purbeck,* Wincanton.

Ed. Lt. Col. R.F. Evans, *Danger Forward; The Story of the First Division In World War 11,* Washington, 1947.

Dorset County Chronicle, 1939 – 1942.

Rodney Legg, *D-Day Dorset,* Wincanton, 1994.

    Dorset At War; Diary of WW2, Wincanton, 1990.

    Dorset Aviation Encyclopaedia, Wincanton, 1996.

    Dorset's War, 1939-45, Wincanton, 1986.

John Murray, *Dorset At War,* Sherborne, 1979.

Chester Wilmot, *The Struggle For The Mastery Of Europe,* 1952.

Unpublished Sources.

William Shaw, *A Biography of Frank Shaw.*

Oral Sources and Memories.

Eddie Anderson; Frank Anderson; Maurie Ash; Ron Axon; Jack Baggs; Bet Best; Monty Best; Percy Best; Archie Brennan; Joan Brien (nee Anderson); Margaret Bugler (nee Green); Harry Clark; Edie Cleal; Dan'l Coombes; Florence Coombes; Charlie Damer; Edie Diamond (nee Joyce); Herbie Elmes; Hughie Elmes; Ken Ford; F. George; Bert Grant; David Grant; Brian Hallett; Ray Herridge; Lois Hibberd (nee Howe); Ethel Kitcat; Doris James (nee Fooks); Marjorie Jeffries (nee Brewer); Ethel Kitcat; Gill Lamb (nee Welsh); Vic Lillington; Phyl Marsh (nee Candy); Emily Newbery; Maud Norris; Beryl Pearce (nee Binding); Harold Rawles; Audrey Richards; June Riggs (nee Thompson); Doris Samways; F. Sargent; Dora and Jean Spence; Jack Spiller; John Symonds; Bob Thompson; Jack Tubbs; Ray Watkins; Ken Wills.

Pamela Jeffries and Lynne Mead at Angleberry Court.

Sue Elmes.

Carl Best; Joe Catt; Bill Costello; Ken Delaney; John Eustace; Angelo Fasano; Bill Lee; Rocky Moretto.

Butch and Joan Jaeger.

Photographs and Illustrations.

The author is very grateful to all those who have lent photographic material. Wherever possible, they have been acknowledged in the text.

"Somewhere In England."

Using some of the memories in this book, Terence has turned them into an absorbing play, called "Somewhere In England," which had considerable success during 2003 in Stafford where the author lives. Further details of this can be had from the author at 2, The Oaks, Kitlings Lane, Stafford, ST17 OLE.